The Convention and Meeting Planner's Handbook

The Convention and Meeting Planner's Handbook

A Step-by-Step Guide
to Making Your Event a Success

Michele Voso

Lexington Books

D.C. Heath and Company/Lexington, Massachusetts/Toronto

Library of Congress Cataloging-in-Publication Data

Voso, Michele.
The convention and meeting planner's handbook: A step-by-step guide to making
your event a success / Michele Voso.
p.   cm.
ISBN 0-669-21153-2 (alk. paper)
1. Meetings—Handbooks, manuals, etc.   2. Congresses and
conventions—Handbooks, manuals, etc.   I. Title.
AS6.V67   1990
658.4′56—dc20   89-39884
                                                                                                      CIP

Published simultaneously in Canada
Printed in the United States of America
Casebound International Standard Book Number: 0-669-21153-2
Library of Congress Catalog Card Number: 89-39884

The paper used in this publication meets the minimum requirements of
American National Standard for Information Sciences—Permanence of
Paper for Printed Library Materials, ANSI Z39.48-1984. ∞™

Year and number of this printing:

92 10 9 8 7 6 5 4 3 2

To Frank, Toni Ann, Bob, Emily, Chris, and
Julian Bach, my agent.

Contents

Figures

Preface

M any years ago, when I first became a meeting planner, people would appear perplexed at my explanations about my job: "I've never seen a job like yours advertised in the paper." "How did you get a job like that?" "You do *what?*"

Today I hear: "I've been planning all the meetings for my company, I love what I do, but I think I'm ready for a bigger challenge. What's it like to manage a convention? Where do I learn the skills? How do I find a job in convention management?"

It was questions like these which led me to write this book. I wanted to isolate convention management from the other types of meeting planning—that for corporate meetings, seminars, incentive meetings, special events—and focus on conventions and trade shows. And since the topic of convention management is so vast, I wanted to go a step further and emphasize on-site management and the crucial eighteen months prior to the opening of a convention, in addition to the actual process involved in choosing a site.

The apparent complexity of on-site convention management is due largely to unfamiliarity with the different types of laborers who are hired and with the way in which the various components of a meeting flow into one another. In truth, the simplicity of meeting management becomes evident when you can step back and view the meeting as you would a work of art: Close up, it reveals dabs of paint; at a distance, it all makes sense. It is the convention manager's job to step back, view the big picture, and decide where the dabs of paint—in this case, the carpenters, plumbers, audiovisual technicians, bus drivers, attendees, and so on—should all be placed to complete the picture.

Having just said that the job is simple, I hasten to add that so is making a soufflé—but you have to know the tricks.

This book should be of use to meeting planners who are currently managing small meetings, corporate meetings, or conventions that have outgrown convention hotels and must now be held in convention centers. The information will add to these persons' meeting-planning skills and help smooth the transition.

The book should also be of use to a host of others—convention and visitors bureau representatives, hotel convention services personnel, service contractors, security firms and others in the business of selling goods and services to meeting planners. Many such companies have lost business because they did not fully understand the job of a convention manager.

Further, travel agents interested in adding meeting planning to the services they offer, multimanagement companies, and convention managers working with colleges and universities to develop courses in convention management will find the book helpful in instructing trainees.

Labor union representatives and city planners who will never manage a meeting themselves will also benefit from seeing the convention industry from a convention manager's viewpoint.

And finally, those career changers who have a variety of skills that can be translated into meeting management expertise, as well as administrators, teachers, secretaries, and others endowed with a mind for detail, leadership qualities, and the ambition and energy to pursue a career, should find this book useful.

In every trade, people develop terms or give unique meanings to standard terms in order to communicate precisely and concisely with one another. To assist the reader, I have defined such pieces of trade jargon the first time they appear in the text; moreover, the glossary in the back of this book defines a range of meeting terms.

Also at the end of the book is a list of suggested readings for those people interested in learning more about convention management as a career or seeking to add to their meeting-planning skills. Finally, in Chapter 12 the reader will find information on organizations and societies whose members and leaders are in the field of meeting planning and convention management.

Acknowledgments

I would like to express my heartfelt thanks to the many persons who gave patient and thoughtful answers to my numerous questions. In particular, special thanks go to the individuals listed below, who volunteered to read and criticize those chapters which covered their area of specialty. Needless to say, the author bears full responsibility for any errors of fact, which I hope are few.

Maribeth Kraus

Larry Rowell

Linda Pilgrim

Roni Feldman-Herberman

Linda Higginson

Dennis Park

Frank Santos

1
Meetings
Overview:
Conventions, Trade Shows,
and Other Types of Meetings

People the world over love to meet. They also love to join groups—groups that have a common interest, like the Water Lily Society, or a not-so-common interest, like the International Brotherhood of Magicians, to cite two examples.

But nowhere in the world outside the United States do people meet on such a large scale—on so large a scale, in fact, that our national preoccupation with meetings has fostered a $40 billion industry to satisfy its needs.

As far back as 1835, Alexis de Tocqueville observed, in *Democracy in America,* that

> Americans of all ages, all conditions, and all dispositions constantly form associations. They have not only commercial and manufacturing companies, in which all take part, but associations of a thousand other kinds, religious, moral, serious, futile, general or restricted, enormous or diminutive. The Americans make associations to give entertainments, to found seminaries, to build inns, to construct churches, to diffuse books, to send missionaries to the antipodes. . . . If it is proposed to inculcate some truth or to foster some feeling by the encouragement of a great example, they form a society.

In other words, they love to meet. And this book is about meetings, large meetings. It is also about meeting planning and meeting planners.

Kinds of Meetings

Some of the more typical kinds of meetings that require special talents and a knowledge of meeting planning include corporate meetings, which can be anything from a board meeting or a shareholders' meeting to a brainstorming session; employee training seminars; and incentive meetings, sponsored by many corporations to award and motivate productive employees.

Then there are the mega-meetings: meetings that are held for thousands of attendees, that are generally referred to as conventions, and that are the kind of meeting that is the focus of this book.

Meeting Planners

Meeting planning is not a field with which most people are familiar, yet many talented, personable individuals would thrive in this industry.

An accurate description of a meeting planner would be Webster's definition of the word *conglomerate*—"made up of separate parts collected together into a single mass." Meeting planners are a collection of paradoxes: punctilious free-wheelers; time-obsessed fanatics with no sense of their own personal clock, unaware that five o'clock has long since come and gone; nitpickers who can see the big picture and develop elaborate, creative special events; and diplomats who shoot from the hip. They are people who feel just as at home in Youngstown, Ohio, munching on the first-prize-winning apple pie at a country fair, as they do riding an elephant in Chiang Mai, Thailand—and both these experiences are possible when one is a meeting planner.

Meeting planners are world travelers, the advance men and women for the companies and organizations they represent, testing, exploring, and absorbing all the sights, sounds, and facilities the world has to offer for conventions and meetings. And few places are left in the world where a meeting has never been held.

Meeting planners take everything in stride but never settle for anything less than the best when it's their meeting that's in town. They love to meet people, and they create an atmosphere in which people love to meet. They're entertainers, negotiators, diplomats, educators, gourmets, and good sports.

Some are highly educated, with the papers to prove it; others are highly educated but haven't a single credential on paper. Some, in past occupations, have been secretaries, accountants, teachers, or advertising account executives; others began as meeting planners and never left the field.

Meeting planners learn to see the world through the eyes of their organizations. And through the knowledge gained in that environment, it becomes second nature to see the world through the eyes of other organizations, groups, political parties, countries, and governments.

The following is an interesting example of how a meeting planner literally must view the world as others view it—or not view it, as in the case of the National Piano Tuners Association. Sounding prosaic enough in it's name, the National Piano Tuners Association consists, naturally, of piano tuners. The fact is that a significant portion of the membership is sight impaired and made up of people who have turned a handicap into an asset. Put yourself in the position of the meeting planner who is responsible for organizing the national annual meeting for this group, and you will understand how a meeting planner is challenged by this organization's requirements.

You will learn, among other things, that many members travel with seeing-eye dogs. Therefore, all the hotels involved with this group must be alerted, well in advance, of the particular and unusual feature of its members. Not only has the meeting planner chosen sites with braille floor indicators in the elevators and emergency instructions in braille, but the planner has also made arrangements for the seeing-eye dogs to be fed, watered, and exercised and has located nearby areas (perhaps even grassy areas) for all the other things dogs do. The hotel staff has also been educated to understand that whereas under ordinary circumstances a room-service tray or cart left on the floor outside a room can be ignored for a time without incident, leaving a tray outside a door when the floor is occupied with sight-impaired individuals can lead to accidents and injuries.

Or take the planner who organized the meetings of the Little People of America. It really didn't make much sense to put anyone on any floor higher than ten—unless of course, the hotel was prepared to hand out wands so that members could reach the buttons for the higher floors, no member being taller than 4 feet. But whatever hotel was chosen, steps had to be specially constructed for all the registration desks to handle the registering members on opening day.

Meetings, Trade Shows, and Conventions

This book is divided into twelve chapters, each addressing a specific element crucial to professional convention management. A meeting, whether it be a trade show or a convention, demands the same skills and knowledge. The difference, however, between a meeting planner and a meeting planner with trade-show experience is that the latter can produce meetings of all sizes, large and small, whereas the former is limited to meetings of small groups.

If the group is quite large—a thousand or more people—it will be referred to in this book as a convention. If the convention has an exhibition consisting of merchandise or other items of interest to the group, it will be referred to as a trade show.

Types of Trade Shows

Professional Trade Shows

Generally speaking, a trade show produced by a professional association or society (medical, scientific, or special interest), will have as its main objective assisting its members and the industry at large in learning about advances in the field, public relations, and, depending on the association, government relations. A professional trade show produced for this type of audience would feature merchandise geared to the group's specific interests—for example, operating-room equipment and accessories for operating-room nurses and surgeons. In addition to the exhibition, educational programs will be planned, offering attendees an opportunity to obtain continuing education credits. Accreditation of continuing medical education is mandatory for physicians and is usually acquired at these large meetings. This type of convention would be announced only to the membership of the association and would not be of interest to the general public. For example, operating-room nurses would see announcements of this show in the monthly journal for operating-room nurses and would receive information through the mail, because they are members of the operating-room nurses' association.

Industry Trade Shows or Public Trade Shows

A trade show produced by manufacturers or dealers of consumer goods will be more interested in selling products to the general public. An industry or public show might be a boat show, an automobile show, a show featuring computer hardware and software, or a camera show and would be advertised to the general public through newspaper ads and TV and radio commercials.

A professional or industry event of this magnitude typically will be held in a large convention center. The Jacob Javits Convention Center in New York City and the McCormick Place Convention Center in Chicago are examples of sites large enough to handle a show of this size.

The Steps Involved in Planning a Convention

The best way to begin to plan and implement an undertaking of this size is to segment the entire process into an orderly array of manageable tasks, which include the following:

- Choosing a suitable city in which to produce the show

- Finding hotel accommodations to house attendees

- Choosing a convention center for the exhibition

- Hiring a destination management company to assist in on-site management

- Arranging for audiovisual equipment

- Arranging in-city transportation

- Planning security needs

- Developing a floor plan of the exhibit hall

- Planning special events

- Directing on-site management

This book explains in detail how to implement these tasks and elaborates on that detail by citing examples, charts, and floor plans.

For instance, chapter 2 not only describes how to develop a request for a proposal to submit to the convention and visitors bureau of a city that could perhaps host an event but also gives an example of a request for a proposal, discusses the economic value to a city of hosting a convention, and offers tips on planning and conducting a citywide site inspection.

Ample, attractive, safe, and clean lodging for convention attendees is the focal point of chapter 3. Finding suitable accommodations and developing a housing block, determining arrival/departure patterns, creating a housing form, working with a housing bureau, and designating a headquarters hotel are some of the topics covered. Formulas for complimentary room allocation are explained, as is an effective strategy for turning your housing form into a negotiating tool.

The nerve center of all conventions is the convention center, the sole topic of chapter 4. Evaluating the property as it relates to a trade show is covered in detail; typical trade-show procedures for scheduling move-in, move-out, and on-site utilities—electrical, water, and compressed air—are discussed and evaluated; calculating square footage, gross and net, are analyzed; and additional information on meeting rooms and accommodations for handicapped attendees is provided.

Chapter 5 addresses the actual staging of a trade show: designing a floor plan and decorating the convention center. Trade unions are defined and union relations discussed. Exhibitor relations and services are also covered, and a little-known but highly successful marketing plan is revealed, with step-by-step information on implementing this exciting sales tool.

A less exciting but crucial element of meeting planning is security and safety. Chapter 6 gives a detailed plan for instituting proper security procedures for the convention center, including flow charts for around-the-clock guard duty. Also covered are the topics of exhibitor security, attendee safety, and show management responsibilities.

Chapter 7 deals exclusively with on-site communications and how to develop an efficient plan for staffing a center of show communications.

In-depth information on working with destination management companies and on handling the logistics of parties for thousands of people, as well as tips on crowd control, is presented in chapter 8.

Chapter 9 maps out an efficient on-site registration area that makes optimum use of space while saving on personnel wear and tear. This chapter also covers exhibitor lead lists, preregistration, and the setting up of attendee service booths for an attractive and functional lobby and gives suggestions for planning an efficient and economical airport shuttle service for the last-day rush.

Chapter 10 focuses on audiovisuals, spelling out the logistics of staging enormous educational programs and explaining the development of a speaker rehearsal room that can be used for programs featuring hundreds of speakers a day.

Chapter 11 outlines, step by step, how to develop and implement an economical and efficient shuttle-bus system, including tips for avoiding the most common pitfalls of meeting planners when devising such a system.

Finally, chapter 12 presents a potpourri of topics—ethical issues, advice on mapping out a career path in meeting and convention management, and courses and organizations for meeting planners.

2
Choosing a City for a Convention

As odd as it may seem, finding a suitable site for a large convention is not so complicated as it first appears. Logistically speaking, when a show reaches a certain size—including delegate population, number of hotel rooms, size of exhibition, and scope of the educational program—the number of suitable sites is narrowed to those cities which have the facilities to handle very large groups of people and which are specifically geared to manage the unique requirements of large conventions.

Two Halves Make a Whole

The two halves referred to in the heading for this section are (a) the meeting planner with a convention looking for a city and (b) the city looking for a meeting planner with a convention. The key to understanding the process of fitting these two halves together is to begin by dividing the two principles, defining them and their various needs and expectations, and then discussing how to mesh the two into a perfect match.

Defining the Basics

Any city wishing to host a large convention must meet certain requirements. A convention with a trade show and educational program will have at least some of—and quite likely even more than—the following basic requirements:

- A convention center with adequate exhibit space
- A sufficient number of meeting rooms in a range of sizes

- Enough sleeping rooms to accommodate delegates and exhibitors

- A suitable hotel to serve as headquarters

- For the balance of the housing, other hotels within walking distance or a short ride to the convention center

- A good selection of sites for special events

- A sufficient number of suppliers of various services: destination management companies to handle special events and shuttle busing, audiovisual equipment suppliers, service contractors, show decorators, and printing and copying companies, to name a few

- A large and varied labor pool for installing and dismantling the exhibition, operating audiovisual equipment, and staffing the registration area and other service desks during the convention

- Adequate air access

These are the highlights a meeting planner would consider when choosing a city as a possible convention site.

With respect to the last item—assessing air access—if the hosting organization is an international society or association, ease of accessibility of non-U.S. delegates must also play a part in the decision. Cities with international airports serviced by several airlines with numerous daily flights into and out of the city would be the first choice of a meeting planner with this type of delegate profile. (Foreign delegates will appreciate avoiding excessive costs and adding further hours to an already-long journey.) By contrast, planners with nonforeign delegates have more flexibility and can take advantage of sites not available to those planners whose foreign membership is sizable.

Armchair Shopping

Many answers to the questions a planner will have about a city's ability to handle a particular convention can be found without leaving the office or talking with anyone. Resource books that deal exclusively with convention sites can be consulted before any contact is made with a city. The *Successful Meetings Sourcebook*[1] is one publication that will answer a great many questions. For instance, under Los Angeles will be listed the following:

- Name, address, and phone number of the convention and visitors bureau

- Names of all the sites suitable for large meetings and conventions—for Los Angeles, the California Mart Exhibit Center, the Los Angeles Convention Center, the Shrine Auditorium and Exposition Center, and the USCAL Davidson Conference Center

- All pertinent information about each site—in the case of the Los Angeles Convention Center, specifications concerning exhibit space, ceiling height, floor load capacity, largest entrance dimensions, number of elevators (freight and passenger), available utilities,number of meeting rooms, kitchen capacities, parking availability, and distance from the city's business district

- All the major hotels, with an equally comprehensive list of specifications

Using the information available in this resource, you can then find out what other large conventions have recently been held in the city by calling the convention and visitors bureau. That information can then be followed up by calling the various associations and speaking with other meeting planners to get an impression of their experience in the city.

The Meeting Industry's City Classifications

There are also general industry evaluations that are given to cities based on some of the above points. Cities are divided into three distinct levels: first-, second-, and third-tier cities.

First-Tier Cities

First-tier cities are considered primary sites for large conventions, having all the resources to accommodate large crowds: one or more large international airports offering hundreds of flights and serviced by many airlines, one or more huge convention centers, thousands of hotel rooms, natural tourist appeal, adequate human resources, industry suppliers (audiovisual companies, show decorating firms, buses for shuttles), and numerous restaurants and attractions. These sites guarantee meeting planners a good turnout at conventions by virtue of their reputation for excitement, beauty, and nightlife. They are expensive cities and will cost a meeting planner more than if the show were to run in a second-tier or third-tier city: Labor, equipment, hotel rooms, and food-and-beverage costs will be more expensive in a first-tier city. The cost of staging a show in one of these cities could be offset, however, by the increased number of delegates that will attend.

A few examples of first-tier cities include Chicago, San Francisco, and New York.

Second-Tier Cities

Second-tier cities are represented by those sites which are not considered primary tourist attractions and which do not have as wide a range of flights, hence may be more difficult and possibly more expensive to reach by air. Although a second-tier city may boast an enormous convention center, enough hotel rooms may not be available or, if available, not within a reasonable distance of the convention center. Additionally, second-tier cities may not offer large hotels that can commit a thousand or fourteen hundred rooms to a meeting planner. Without these large hotels, a meeting planner is forced to seek housing in numerous hotels that are able to commit only a few hundred rooms each.

When Second-Tier Cities Are a Wise Alternative

If a meeting planner is willing to work with the city and be flexible about housing-block arrangements, second-tier cities can offer wonderful advantages that are not always available when shows are held in more glamorous cities.

Second-tier cities, being smaller, will offer a friendly and intimate atmosphere, with great dollar savings to both the meeting planner and the delegate that cannot be expected from a large city like New York or San Francisco. Choosing a city like Toronto or Minneapolis for a show will put you in the admirable position of being the only show in town, whereas in New York or San Francisco your show could be (and quite often is) just one of many that are taking place at the same time.

Third-Tier Cities

While third-tier cities might make excellent destinations for innumerable meetings, they are not considered satisfactory sites for large conventions, inasmuch as their air access, hotel rooms, meeting-room space, and human resources are limited for serving the needs of such conventions. The situation is changing, however, and many previously unsuitable sites are entering the competition for large convention business.

Narrowing the Field

Many organizations plan their annual meetings on a rotational basis, following an east-middle-west pattern that greatly narrows the choices. The lead time between booking a convention and the actual even is typically seven to ten years. Therefore, a planner for a large convention will not be faced with an overwhelming schedule of site inspections and will most likely be viewing cities that have already hosted the convention in the past.

The Other Half of the Equation

To get a well-rounded view of the selection process, it is helpful to understand the convention from a city's perspective. Why would a city want to attract conventions? Money—clean, or what is sometimes referred to as smokeless, dollars.

Economic Value of a Convention

A survey conducted by the International Association of Convention bureaus in 1988[1] indicated that an individual convention delegate generated an average of $787.54 in direct income to the host city, based on an average stay of four nights. This figure does not include expenditures by the meeting organization, exhibitors, and service contractors. That means that a convention that attracts seven thousand attendees, four thousand of them delegates, can bring the city approximately $3 million. Add to that figure the amount of money that is spent by exhibitors who do the following:

- Hire workers to install and dismantle exhibits

- Hire service contractors to decorate exhibits

- Use hundreds of hotel rooms to house sales staff and technical staff to service equipment

- Spend money on special events, parties, and hospitality suites to entertain delegates

- Use all the services of hotels and a city that a delegate would use, such as room service, cabs, and restaurants

And all of this does not take into consideration the money spent by the exhibiting organization to stage the event: renting the facility, using prodigious amounts of labor, and giving a great deal of business to local suppliers and merchants. All together, a medium-size show with approximately seven thousand attendees could easily, in four- or five-day period, bring a city anywhere from $10 to 12 million. It appears that the cure for many a city beset by unemployment and a deteriorating downtown is to build a convention center and get into the convention business. And that cure seems to be working.

Standard Operating Procedures

Certain traditional procedures should be followed when investigating a city as a possible convention site. These steps include (a) preparing a request for a proposal, (b) contacting a convention and visitors bureau, (c) planning and arranging a site inspection, and (d) following up with a decision.

Preparing a Request for a Proposal

You will need to develop specifications about a show before alerting a city to your interest in it as a possible site. A *request for a proposal* is a statement of activity that defines the meeting and its functions and that is used by a convention and visitors bureau to determine whether a convention can be accommodated by the city for the requested dates and size of the show.

A comprehensive specification sheet will include the following elements:

- Statement about the organization and its primary goals or business, including a delegate profile

- Preferred and optional dates

- Number of delegates and comparison of several years' attendance figures

- Number of hotel rooms needed

- Arrival/departure pattern

- Activities

- Number of exhibiting companies

- Move-in/move-out schedule

- Exhibition dates

- Ancillary meeting information

- Headquarters hotel specifications

- Breakdown of room types

- Convention center specifications

- Information on how to submit a proposal

When all the pieces are put into place, a typical request for a proposal will take the following shape:

Request for a Proposal for the 1996 Annual Meeting

To: Convention and visitors bureau
From: Meeting planner
Effective Date: 8/9/89
General Information
　　The organization is composed of approximately 10,000 members. The annual meeting draws a total attendance of approximately 7,000 people, categorized as follows:

	Head Count		
	1988	*1987*	*1986*
Professionals	1,813	1,631	1,468
Semiprofessionals	947	852	767
Administrators	1,147	1,032	929
Exhibitors	1,500	1,350	1,215
Spouses, press, and so on	468	444	422
Commercial professionals	1,215	1,093	984
Total	7,090	6,402	5,785

There is an estimated 8 percent growth for the 1990 program.

Preferred Dates

First choice: Second week of June
Second choice: First week of June
Third choice: Third week of June
Fourth choice: last two weeks of May

Housing Arrival/Departure Pattern

	Number of Rooms
First Monday	10
First Tuesday	14
First Wednesday	30
First Thursday	200
First Friday	400
First Saturday	600
First Sunday	2,000
Second Monday	3,100
Second Tuesday	3,200
Second Wednesday	3,100
Second Thursday	2,000
Second Friday	800
Second Saturday	70
Second Sunday	15

The activities of the annual meeting consist of the following:

Activity	Day(s)
Move-in	First Wednesday–Second Monday
20 committee meetings at headquarters, ranging in size from 15 to 30, conference style	First Friday
1 national board meeting at headquarters	First Saturday
60 committee meetings at headquarters, ranging in size from 15 to 25, conference style	First Sunday
1 local board meeting at headquarters	Second Monday
6 premeeting seminars at headquarters	Second Monday
Official show dates at the convention center	Second Tuesday–Second Friday

There are approximately 115 technical exhibits, consisting of three 50-by-90-foot islands, several 40-by-50-foot islands, and many 20-by-20 and 10-by-10-foot booths. Also included on the exhibit floor are several hundred posters encompassing approximately 10,000 square feet of exhibit floor space.

These show dates will include the following:

- 87 educational paper sessions (there are 6 educational paper sessions, presented orally in each session; the program runs for 5 days, with a total of 544 orally presented papers)

- 21 continuing education courses at the convention center

- 10 special symposia (workshops, panels, and so on) at the convention center

- Move-out   Second Friday–second Saturday (12:00 midnight)

Headquarters Hotel

Traditionally, a hotel is designated as headquarters and houses the committee meetings, board meetings, and most social functions.

Space Preferred	Days
1,400 Sleeping rooms and approximately 60 suites	Same as overall arrival/departure with higher pickup on the first Saturday
1 Convention office (approximately 2,000 square feet)	First Wednesday–second Saturday
20 Committee meetings for 15–30, conference style (need minimum of 8 rooms)	First Friday
1 Board meeting set for 40 hollow square[a] and 75 theater style	First Saturday
60 Committee meetings 15–25, conference style (need minimum of 14 rooms)	First Sunday
Icebreaker reception[b] 3,000-capacity ballroom	Second Monday
Exhibitors' party: 3,000-capacity ballroom	Second Thursday

[a]See glossary for description of hollow square and theater style.
[b]The icebreaker reception attracts approximately 2,500 guests and offers a cash bar, dry snacks, entertainment, and dancing.

The exhibitors' party is a themed event with entertainment and dancing, a hosted bar, and a buffet dinner for approximately 2,800. (By annotating food-and-beverage requirements in this manner, you will be giving the convention and visitors bureau all the necessary information to ensure that space for these large functions is available. Although a site may have dates available for the convention center and enough hotel rooms to satisfy housing needs, local events and parties may have a hold on large function space.)

Lunches will be served for a majority of the committees on both days they meet. Lunches will be served for approximately 100 on the board meeting day,and refreshments will be served throughout the day on both committee meeting days.

In addition to the above space needs and depending on meeting space at headquarters, a hold of additional space for the use of groups convening in conjunction with the organization's annual meeting will also be required. Generally, many exhibiting companies sponsor one or more meetings, receptions, and special events, and related associations will convene concurrently with the annual meeting.

A complete list of exhibitors will be distributed to all properties and suppliers one year prior to the event at an exhibitor/supplier/hotel preview meeting.

Breakdown of Room Types

Room Type	Number
Singles	2,112
Doubles/twins	992
Triples	32
Quads	25
1-bedroom suites	39
Total	3,200

Site Decision

The site decision is made at one of two board meetings held each year. The meeting planner makes suggestions about the site and then presents the information to the board for a vote. The convention and visitors bureau representative may be asked to make a presentation at the board meeting preceding the one in which the decision is made. In the case of the 1996 meeting, the decision is scheduled for February 1990.

Convention Center Specifications

Space Preferred	Day(s)
150,000 gross square feet of exhibit space: 100,000 for commercial exhibits, 20,000 for noncommercial exhibits, 20,000 for concessions and storage, and 10,000 for growth[a]	First Wednesday–second Saturday
2 convention offices 2 press offices 1 accounting office 2 audiovisual/audiotaping offices 3 conference rooms (30–35 people) 1 exhibitors' lounge 1 speaker rehearsal room	First Wednesday–second Saturday (11 days)
8 seminars for 1,000, 1,000, 800, 800, 400, 400, 200, and 200	Second Monday
1 plenary session[b] for 2,000, theater style, with extensive audiovisuals	Second Tuesday
9 sessions for 1,000, 900, 900, 800, 500, 500, 400, 400, and 300, theater style	Second Tuesday–second Friday

[a]Many large shows are booked a minimum of five—and more likely, seven to ten—years in advance. This figure allows a cushion for growth and can be updated and revised from year to year after the show is booked.

[b]The plenary session is the opening-day event. It is followed by a sound-and-light video display that immediately precedes the opening of the exhibit hall. Food-and-beverage requirements for the entire five days are—in addition to the concession stands—exhibitor-sponsored coffee breaks every morning and afternoon (the morning break offers parties) and exhibitor-sponsored buffet luncheons for three days.

To Respond to this Proposal Please Send the Following to (name/address).

From the convention center:

- Floor plan with capacities
- Sample or actual contract
- Specification of the exact space that is being held on a daily basis

From the hotels or convention bureau:

- List of hotels available and committable rooms being held on a daily basis

- City map showing various shuttle-bus routes
- Information on attractions, restaurants, and so on
- List of local suppliers

Contacting a Convention and Visitors Bureau

Where should you send a request for a proposal? When dealing with large conventions, the traditional path is to contact the convention and visitors bureau in the city that is being considered.

Most likely, a representative from the bureau will contact you immediately upon receipt of your documents. He or she will have already checked to see whether the preferred dates are free at the convention center and whether a sufficient number of hotel rooms are available during those dates to meet your requirements. Arrangements will then be made for scheduling an inspection.

Planning and Arranging a Site Inspection

Typically, the convention bureau representative will be the one to arrange the scheduling of a site inspection. Working together, both meeting planner and bureau representative will determine the likely hotels to visit and what special sites to inspect for possible nonhotel special events for the hosting organization and exhibitors.

Site inspections for citywide conventions are quite involved, and ample time must be sent with the bureau representative to ensure that all practicable hotel properties are examined and that sufficient time is allocated to thoroughly inspect the convention center.

It is not unusual for a meeting planner to tour three hotels in the morning, have lunch at a fourth, tour three more in the afternoon, dine at still another, and follow this type of schedule for two or more days.

The extent of each tour of each hotel can be determined only by the meeting planner. If one or several hotels are likely candidates for headquarters, a more in-depth tour involving meeting rooms, large function space, and suites would be called for, as would seeing the various types and sizes of sleeping rooms.

Hotels that will primarily be used for overflow—that is, for housing only—will require less scrutiny. Additionally, if the meeting in question will not take place for another seven to ten years, anything more than just a quick sweep of the sleeping accommodations and public space would be a waste of time, since most likely the property will have undergone renovations between the time of the site inspection and the actual meeting. (*Note:* The typical procedure for holding space for meetings of this size and working with a seven- to ten-year time frame is to tentatively hold space until a time closer to the date of the show, when the sites can be reinspected and definite contracts entered into. See chapter 3 for more extensive information on housing.)

Keeping Exhibitors' Needs in Mind. Additional time should be allocated during a site inspection to view nonhotel sites for exhibitor-sponsored special events. Such sites include a wide range of properties,such as museums, art galleries, amusement parks, private estates, and municipal zoos, as well as an endless array of other exciting places that make wonderful sites for themed parties and receptions.

Arranging for an Adequate Time Cushion with the Convention Center. In addition to the site inspection information on convention centers that is detailed in chapter 4, time should be spent with the center's representative discussing the particular characteristics of your show and examining the center's schedule of events that surround your show.

In the preliminary specification sheet that was submitted as a request for a proposal, a *space* cushion was added to the requirements to allow for possible growth of the show's exhibition. A *time* cushion should also be discussed with the center's representative—not only your show's move-in/move-out time schedule but also that of the events immediately preceding and following your show. A tight schedule could cause problems in the future if your show and those preceding and following it expand in the number of days required for their move-in and move-out.

Following Up with a Decision

The decision to book a city is not usually left solely to the meeting planner. A decision of this magnitude is typically left to a board or to a site selection committee.

Courtesy dictates that the decision not be put off indefinitely. It is also important to keep the convention and visitors bureau advised of any changes in the size of your exhibit space, the number of delegates, the number and size of food-and-beverage functions, or the arrival/departure patterns, as well as any change in the projected decision date.

3
The Building Blocks of a Housing Plan

Whether a meeting planner needs three thousand, ten thousand, or five hundred rooms to house attendees, the process of acquiring rooms and setting up a system that flows into the entire meeting plan entails several stages. Developing a tentative housing block is the first step and the foundation from which all the other tasks progress.

Developing a Tentative Housing Block

Most major conventions use several hotels to accommodate attendees. Although hotels large enough to offer a meeting planner thousands of rooms do exist, such an arrangement is not usually the case. If three thousand rooms are needed, they are distributed among several hotels. Hotels that have only five hundred rooms will be able to *commit*, or offer, only a portion of those rooms to the meeting planner, the balance being reserved for transient and other customers. Consequently, meeting planners must develop a housing block to accommodate attendees. The phrase *housing block* refers to the number of rooms a meeting planner will hold aside in one or several hotels in the convention city to provide guaranteed housing for an event's participants.

Making a Commitment

For the purpose of illustration, let's assume that (a) booking several hotels is necessary to achieve the desired number of rooms in a housing block and (b) three thousand is the number of rooms necessary to house attendees.

Most housing blocks begin with commitments from many hotels, totaling more rooms than are actually needed for the block. A review of the various hotel commitments will reveal a total of perhaps four thousand rooms that are available to a group at the time of the convention. Since you can hope to fill only three thousand of those rooms, you must decide which hotels best suit your needs and eliminate the rest.

The following points should be noted when deciding on hotels for a housing block:

- Location of each hotel in relation to the convention center
- Location of each hotel in relation to the other hotels on the block
- Range of rates offered in each hotel
- Range of rates offered in the overall block
- Types of rooms available

Location of Hotels to the Convention Center

Hotel location should be given top priority, since other aspects of your planning hinge directly on this factor. In many cities, the convention center is not in the heart of the city, for these centers are large structures requiring extensive tracts of land that would be prohibitively expensive in a city's hub. Moreover, convention centers are occasionally viewed as disruptive to vehicular and pedestrian traffic.

Preferably, the trip from any hotel in the housing block to the convention center should take no more than ten to twelve minutes by shuttle bus and ideally should be within walking distance. Too great a distance from the convention center to the hotels will increase the cost of shuttle-bus service. (For a discussion of shuttle-bus systems, see chapter 11.)

Location of Hotels to One Another

The need to keep all hotels in close proximity to one another, like the need to keep hotels near the convention center, is based on the desire to save on the cost of shuttle busing.

Range of Rates in Each Hotel

What delegates are able to pay for hotel rooms is determined by examining the group's profile. Naturally, a group of lawyers, physicians, or engineers will require accommodations suitable to their tastes and will usually be willing and able to pay for comfort, luxury, and amenities. Not all the groups, however, want or need first-class accommodations, and hotels for the event should be chosen accordingly.

Range of Rates in the Housing Block

Your event will, of course, involve a mix of professionals willing to pay for service and, depending on the nature and scope of your show, may also attract attendees related to the profession but representing many other ranks. A range of room rates would thus be necessary to accommodate all attendees in such a group.

Types of Rooms

The various types of rooms—singles, doubles, double-doubles (two double beds), and suites—and classes of rooms—that is, standard accommodations, no view, a long walk to the elevator, and back-of-house versus luxury level accommodations—must be segmented within each property.

Finalizing the Housing Block

For simplicity's sake, assume that the four thousand available rooms are distributed among eight hotels. After you have conducted the site inspections and discussed the rates, your list of candidates will look something like this:

Hotel	Number of Rooms	Rate Range	Accepted
1	1,400	$ 92–140	Yes
2	700	105–165	Yes
3	600	125–185	Yes
4	400	75–105	Yes
5	300	95–110	Yes
6	200	85–115	No
7	200	90–120	No
8	200	145–205	No

The room block is now complete. Hotels 1, 2, 3, 4, and 5 are the choice. These hotels are either within safe walking distance of the convention center or a short shuttle trip away. A site inspection of all the properties has assured you that these hotels offer suitable lodging for attendees, that rates represent a nice range, and that room types are distributed to accommodate the group's needs.

Determining Arrival/Departure Patterns

The hotels will want to know just how to distribute these rooms over the period of your show. Not all three thousand people will appear at the same time on the same day, nor will the hotel holding four hundred rooms for a group have the same arrival pattern as the one holding fourteen hundred rooms. Preshow personnel will be arriving ahead of time to set up the convention center. The show decorator, or service contractor, will be one of the first in town, along with his or her staff; the audiovisual supervisor and crew will also be in early to set up meeting rooms at the convention center. All will need a place to stay. But although a professional organization's leadership may come in a few days earlier to hold business meetings, the bulk of your attendees will arrive the day before the show and in most cases leave immediately after. A check of the housing data concerning the organization's previous shows will supply a good basis to begin working on the arrival/departure pattern for the present show.

A Typical Arrival/Departure Pattern

First using the hypothetical three-thousand-room figure as distributed among the listed hotels and then using the hotel with the largest room block (fourteen hundred rooms) as an example, you can develop an arrival/departure pattern based on the following criteria:

- Number of show days: 4

- Number of preshow meeting days (the business meeting days of the organization's leadership): 4, with day 4 of the preshow meeting days overlapping with day 1 of opening day

- Beginning of preshow meetings: Sunday

- Opening day: Wednesday, with the show running through Saturday

    The resultant pattern would be as follows:

Saturday	Sunday	Monday	Tuesday	Wednesday	Thursday	Friday	Saturday	Sunday
150	300	500	1,200	1,400	1,400	1,000	500	150

On the first Saturday, exhibitors and staff will be coming into town; the leadership of the association will then follow, with the bulk of general attendees arriving the afternoon before opening day. Not all attendees will stay for the entire show—some will leave earlier. Friday's figure reflects that drop, and the figure for the final day of the show, Saturday, reveals that most of the people will have checked out, with a few remaining to check out the morning after the last day. The last figure, for Sunday, represents the original setup personnel remaining for the final move-out.

Determining Distribution by Type of Room

When calculating arrival/departure patterns for each individual hotel, keep in mind that not all rooms will be only single or only double occupancy. Some members of the group will be traveling with a spouse or sharing the room with a friend. Using the event's past history, determine as best you can how many single-occupancy, double-occupancy, and double-occupancy rooms were actually used.

A word about determining suite needs: Many organizations will hold suites in the housing block to accommodate exhibitors' needs for receptions and for hospitality suites in which to entertain attendees. Therefore, estimates must be made of the number of suites in each hotel that will be needed for exhibitors. Most meeting planners control the allocation of suites and ask that the hotel seek the planner's approval for any suite requests.

Establishing a Cutoff Date

A *cutoff date* is the date that a hotel may release any rooms remaining in the housing block that are unsold.

When dealing with numerous hotels, you will not always find it easy to get all of them to decide on one cutoff date. The dates in various contracts can range from two to six weeks before the opening day of the show or from two to six weeks before the first arrival date in a particular hotel's arrival/departure pattern. And some cutoff dates are calculated to include weekends, while others are based on business days.

You will most likely find, upon reading the various contracts, that all the dates are within a few days of one another and that a simple adjustment to the relevant paragraph in the contract is all that is needed.

Process and Product: Developing a Housing Form

Notifying attendees about the accommodations is most easily handled by developing a *housing form*. This form is usually mailed to prospective participants with the first announcement of the show, along with registration materials. The housing form is filled out and mailed directly either to the association's office, if housing is handled directly by the association, or to a housing bureau. (A housing bureau is a department of a convention and visitor's bureau. It is staffed by persons familiar with the technicalities of managing the accommodations for large groups. The service is usually offered at no charge to the exhibiting organization.)

The housing form should communicate all the information that attendees need to select a hotel in their price range or taste. Also included should be data about the cost of cots and cribs, parking availability, and sales and room occupancy taxes, as well as a map to indicate the location of the hotel in relation to the convention center and the other hotels in the housing block.

The example of a housing form in figure 3–1 is just one of many varieties and includes information besides that outlined above. The form has been used for several major conventions attracting more than six thousand attendees and by several housing bureaus that have each found it efficient and easy to work with.

Working with a Housing Bureau

The value that a housing bureau offers to a meeting planner is almost incalculable and represents an economic windfall to the meeting planner who knows how to take advantage of a bureau's many services and staff expertise concerning each hotel's housing policies.

Knowledge is Power

Since housing bureaus have no allegiance to any particular property but do have extensive experience in dealing with many properties, they are in a unique po-

HOUSING REQUEST FORM

TUESDAY–FRIDAY, JUNE 13–16, 1989, ST. LOUIS, MISSOURI

FOR HOUSING BUREAU USE ONLY

PLEASE READ BOTH SIDES CAREFULLY

MAIL TO:

Housing Bureau
10 South Broadway, Suite 300
St. Louis, Missouri 63102

PART I

INSTRUCTIONS: Complete requested data using abbreviations as necessary.

NAME OF PERSON REQUESTING ROOMS

FIRST NAME   LAST

NAME OF COMPANY OR FIRM

STREET ADDRESS OR P.O. BOX NUMBER

CITY   STATE   ZIP

COUNTRY   AREA CODE   PHONE NUMBER

See reverse side for room rates and hotel locations and codes. Please **PRINT** or **TYPE** all items to assure accuracy. Complete each part below in detail for correct and rapid computer processing. Should more than **TWO (2)** rooms be needed, form may be duplicated, or supplemental room list **MUST** be attached using same format as in Part III. **ALL** confirmations will be sent to individual indicated in Part I. All reservations will be processed on a first-come, first-served basis. Either secure your first night by filling in credit card information on this form or mail check to the SNM Housing Bureau no later than May 2, 1989 at the above address.

☐ Please check here if you are disabled and have special requirements.

Reservations must be received by the Housing Bureau no later than May 2, 1989.

PART II

INSTRUCTIONS: Select **THREE** Hotels of your choice. No request will be processed without **THREE** choices. Write in your choices in the space provided on the right.

1st Choice _____

2nd Choice _____

3rd Choice _____

PART III

INSTRUCTIONS: 1. **PRINT** or **TYPE** names of **ALL** persons occupying each room. 2. Select type room desired with arrival and departure dates. 3. Supplemental list for additional room **MUST** use same format. 4. Print or type last name first.

	OCCUPANTS NAME/S (PRINT LAST NAME FIRST)	P + 1: Parlor & one bedroom P + 2: Parlor & two bedrooms	
ROOM NO. 1	1 _____ 2 _____ 3 _____ 4 _____	CHECK ONE ☐ SINGLE ☐ P+1 ☐ DOUBLE ☐ TWIN ☐ P+2 ☐ TRIPLE ☐ QUAD	ARR. DATE _____ DEP. DATE _____ ARRIVAL TIME ___ ☐ AM ☐ PM (Check One) To assure your reservation, a one night's deposit guaranteed by either acceptable credit card or by check (to be credited to your account) must be received by the Housing Bureau no later than May 2 to reserve your room.
ROOM NO. 2	1 _____ 2 _____ 3 _____ 4 _____	CHECK ONE ☐ SINGLE ☐ P+1 ☐ DOUBLE ☐ TWIN ☐ P+2 ☐ TRIPLE ☐ QUAD	ARR. DATE _____ DEP. DATE _____ ARRIVAL TIME ___ ☐ AM ☐ PM (Check One) To assure your reservation, a night's deposit guaranteed by either acceptable credit card or by check (to be credited to your account) must be received by the Housing Bureau no later than May 2 to reserve your room.

I wish to pay by: check ☐ (MADE PAYABLE TO HOUSING BUREAU)

I wish to pay with the following credit card: ☐ American Express   ☐ VISA   ☐ MasterCard

Credit Card Number: _____ Expiration Date: _____ Signature: _____

Housing arrangements are being coordinated by the   Housing Bureau. Application for hotel accommodations should be made to the Housing Bureau. **No reservations will be accepted over the phone.** As far as possible, accommodation will be provided at the hotel of your choice. If this is not possible, you will be assigned comparable accommodation at one of the other hotels. Confirmation of accommodation will be sent to you directly from the hotel to which you have been assigned. Any changes are to be made directly with hotel. Please read hotel confirmations carefully for correct arrival/departure dates and cancellation information.

Figure 3–1. *Housing request form*

28

Name of Hotel, Map Code	Single (1 person, 1 bed)	Double (2 persons, 1 bed)	Twin (2 persons, 2 beds)	One-bedroom suite	Two-bedroom suite	Other	Room Service gratuity added to bill (%) automatically	Extra beds	Parking	Phone Calls
Adam's Mark (Headquarters)	$90.00	$100.00	$100.00			Concierge $125.00 (s) $145.00 (dbl)	18%	$15 per night	$8 per 24 hours $10 valet	.60 per call upon completion
Sheraton St. Louis	$86.00	$99.00 add'l adult $15	$99.00	$350 and up	$500 and up	Hospitality $410–450	$2 delivery charge	no charge	$8 per 24 hours	.60 per call long distance
Drury Inn	$63.00	$63.00	$63.00	69.00 and up		Children under 18 no charge		$8.00	compli-mentary	local calls no charge
Holiday Inn Riverfront	$69.00	$79.00	$79.00	$99 and up		Hospitality $300 and up Child under 17 no charge	not added to bill	no charge	compli-mentary	.50 local $1 per min. long distance
Radisson	$73.00	$83.00	$83.00			Child under 17 no charge	15%	$10	$5 per 24 hours	.50 per call upon completion
Clarion	$74.00	$74.00	$74.00			Child under 17 no charge	16%	$15 per night	$7.50 per 24 hours	.60 per call upon completion
Marriott Pavilion	$99.00	$99.00	$99.00	$400 and up	$500 and up	Concierge $125 and up	17%	$15 cribs free	$10 per 24 hours	.50 direct .75 assisted
Omni International	$84.00	$94.00	$94.00				17%	$20 each	$8 per 24 hours	.60 after 5 rings

HOTEL DESCRIPTIONS

1 Adam's Mark
The Adam's Mark Hotel is a new, 4-Star, 4-Diamond luxury meeting hotel located directly across from St. Louis' Gateway Arch, only six blocks from Cervantes Center.

2 Sheraton St. Louis
Located adjacent to the Cervantes Convention Center, this contemporary hotel has a dramatic atrium lobby lounge with live entertainment, fitness center, outdoor pool and gift shop on the property.

3 Drury Inn
Located adjacent to fabulous Union Station, the Drury Inn retains the elegance of the 1907 Railroad YMCA building which it occupies. Large fireplaces, leaded-glass windows and wood paneling create a warm atmosphere. Free continental breakfast and 4 star gourmet restaurant.

4 Holiday Inn Riverfront
Located in the heart of downtown St. Louis, directly across from the Gateway Arch, the Holiday Inn is within easy walking distance of the Cervantes Center, Busch Stadium and Laclede's Landing. The Holiday Inn offers newly renovated, oversized rooms, some with full-size kitchens.

5 Radisson
Adjacent to the Cervantes Center, with indoor swimming pool, whirlpool, and atrium. The Radisson offers outstanding cuisine, and a service-minded staff.

6 Clarion
A full-service convention hotel, located in the heart of downtown St. Louis. The revolving rooftop restaurant is excellent for lunch or dinner, offering a panoramic view of the city. The Clarion features outdoor and indoor pools, health club and indoor jogging track.

7 Marriott Pavilion
The St. Louis Marriott Pavilion, located two blocks from the Arch and across the street from Busch Stadium, offers a complete exercise facility, indoor pool and a sports bar that is the hot spot for downtown.

8 Omni International
Located within the St. Louis Union Station, a national landmark and marketplace, featuring an outdoor pool, 24-hour room service, two restaurants and two lounges in an elegant atmosphere.

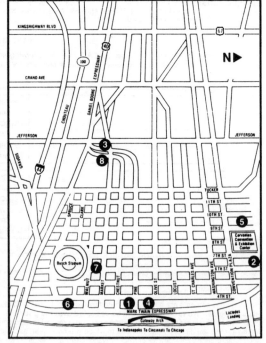

Figure 3–1. *continued*

sition to advise meeting planners about housing policies—for example, whether a hotel will be flexible in fitting in late arrivals at the convention rate, how it handles cancellations and substitutions, and other information not normally made known to a meeting planner. Housing bureau staff members are also experienced in processing thousands of housing requests a year and in dealing with unhappy attendees and authoritative VIPs. All these highly qualified human resources are offered usually at no cost to the organization holding a meeting in the city.

When should you begin working with a housing bureau? To take full advantage of its experience, ideally you should start working with a housing bureau before you begin the final selection of hotels for the housing block.

Working with a Housing Bureau to Develop a Housing Form

Consulting with the housing bureau before beginning plans for a housing form will help you create a form that is compatible with the procedures followed by that particular bureau. Your form will also fit in easily with the bureau's computer programs (or, if the system is not computerized, with the bureau's set procedures) for processing housing requests.

How Housing Bureaus Allocate Hotel Rooms

The process used by housing bureaus to allocate sleeping rooms is based on the housing form. Once that form is mailed to the bureau, the bureau assigns rooms based on request and availability. Usually the bureau mails a preliminary confirmation to the attendee and sends a copy to the hotel. The hotel then reconfirms the accommodation.

Final Room Allocations

The usual procedure a housing bureau will follow for handling requests for rooms in hotels that are completely booked is to assign the registrant to a hotel that still has rooms available. The decision regarding which hotel is used is based on location; that is, the bureau assigns rooms in various hotels according to their proximity to the convention center.

By requesting that the housing bureau use specific hotels with the largest number of remaining rooms, instead of assigning rooms by location, the meeting planner will gain more control over complimentary room allocations and hotels will be filled up in an orderly manner.

Room Pickup Reports

Housing bureaus send meeting planners monthly reports listing room pickup figures for each hotel. As the meeting draws closers, the bureau sends weekly reports. These reports are used to determine whether more rooms are needed or, if the pickup looks to be less than anticipated, to release some rooms.

The final pickup report will also help determine next year's housing needs and can be used to develop requests for proposals for other cities for future meetings.

Verifying Final Housing Figures: A Critical Task

For every convention in every city, the final figures for total room nights are reported to a central data repository administered by the International Association of Convention and Visitors Bureaus (IACVB). It is therefore extremely important for meeting planners to verify that those final figures are accurate. (Room nights refer to the total number of nights actually used for each room sold. If twenty-five reservations are made for three nights and another twenty-five are made for five nights in a block of fifty rooms, the total room night count for that block is $25 \times 3 = 75$ plus $25 \times 5 = 125$, or 225 room nights.)

Inaccurate room counts can affect meeting planners in many ways. As discussed in chapter 2, when a meeting planner decides that a city may be suitable for an event, he or she sends a request for a proposal to the city's convention and visitors bureau; the request includes, among other things, the number of room nights that the event normally sells. If the meeting planner's figures conflict with and are lower than the figures on files at the IACVB, the planner's veracity is questioned and his or her negotiating position jeopardized. With an average four-day show and a three-thousand-room block, for example, selling all three thousand rooms with a total of sixteen thousand room nights is not the same as selling only twenty-five hundred rooms and ten thousand room nights. The show's financial impact, perceived as excellent in the eyes of the meeting planner, may be viewed as less than desirable by the city and the hotels.

Nevertheless, most such misperceptions and misreportings are usually an expression of a meeting planner's inexperience with the workings of housing bureaus and hotels and may also reflect attendees' behavior when making their housing arrangements. Many registrants, for example, will fail to identify themselves as being with a convention group when calling a hotel to make a reservation; the planner does not get credit for this room, nor does the attendee get the discount rate. (This problem does not normally occur when a housing bureau is making reservations; however, when only one or two hotels are involved, a meeting planner may opt not to use a bureau and instead have attendees deal directly with the properties.) The misperceptions and misreportings may also indicate a failure to develop a procedure to ensure the proper accounting of information to all parties involved.

Admittedly, more work has to be done by all—organizations, hotels, meeting planners, housing bureaus, and the IACVB—to come to an equitable solution. Until such time, meeting planners can ease the situation somewhat by enlisting the help and cooperation of the housing bureau and all the hotels on the housing block to achieve an accurate accounting of the housing figures.

Using the Housing Form as a Negotiating Tool

Quite by accident, I discovered a surprising alternative use for the housing form: using it as a tool to negotiate room rates.

Merely wishing to explain why I was requesting a twenty-five-word description of a hotel and wanting to describe the rebate statement on my housing form, I showed the previous year's form to the sales manager of a hotel I was considering for my housing block. He seemed a bit shocked that his rates, as well as those of all the other hotels, would be displayed so comparatively on the form and was also greatly concerned about his hotel's position in the lineup. Until that time, I had always let the housing bureau number the hotels, based on location, as well as prepare the numbered map that appears on the housing form. I usually numbered the hotels based on the housing bureau's map numbers, the only exception being to give the headquarters hotel top billing.

I proceeded to question the sales manager as to how I would otherwise inform attendees of rates, extra costs, and room types that were now available in a practical display. He replied that he didn't know how but that his rates were several dollars higher than the rest, and all the descriptions of the hotels being of a flattering nature, he felt an attendee would tend to choose by rate, not by property. I agreed that this was possible but said, "This is the way it's done." I asked whether he could offer any suggestions other than changing my entire housing form. He suggested lowering his rate. I agreed that this was a good suggestion.

As to an individual hotel's position on the form, I most often use the housing bureau's location (proximity to the convention center) when possible.

Inspecting Hotels

All hotels on the block must be inspected before you contract with any property. These inspections are usually performed eighteen months to a year prior to the show; conducting them any earlier will defeat the purpose of the visit.

Besides the obvious points of cleanliness and overall maintenance, attention should concentrate on public space, especially in the case of the hotel that holds the largest block of rooms (in our example, hotel 1, with fourteen hundred rooms), and how that public space relates to convention management.

Although not all fourteen hundred people will appear at one time, you can expect the major influx of people on the day preceding the show to number a thousand. The lobby should be large enough to handle this kind of crowd.

Guest Registration

An important feature of any hotel being considered for a large block is how it is set up to handle the arrivals and departures of large groups of people. Look for the following:

- *Computerized check-in.* Few hotels in major convention cities are not yet computerized at their registration desks. But if there are not enough terminals to handle the number of check-ins for a large convention, you will have problems. Some hotels, expecting a large group all on the same day, will set up temporary terminals to speed up the registration process.

- *Enough elevators.* The best of all layouts for elevators is to have several banks for set floors—three or four elevators going from floor 1 to 9, another three or four from floor 10 to 18, and so on, in addition to service elevators for bellhops with luggage carts and waiters with room-service trays. If there are not enough elevators, it could take hours for hundreds of people to get to their rooms. If you have arranged with the convention service manager of the hotel to set up extra terminals to quickly process registering guests but there are not enough elevators to get them to their rooms, you have created a double dilemma for yourself. It's best to forget the extra terminals and set up refreshment stands to distract guests while they await their turn at the registration desk than to have them crowding to get into elevators.

Fire Safety and Attendee Safety

A primary responsibility of meeting planners is the safety and security of attendees. It is essential that a planner become familiar with the fire and safety regulations of the convention city. Although fire and safety regulations are of prominent importance in most major cities, they are by no means to be taken for granted. (I once inspected a beautiful, modern facility on a Caribbean island that had no smoke detectors or sprinkler systems and had a narrow, wooden staircase that couldn't possibly accommodate an emergency flow of traffic. Although the property was impressive in every other respect, I had no choice but to reject it.)

The best way to proceed is to observe the surroundings and ask questions. Your questions should provoke a stream of information regarding fire safety. Most hotels are proud of their safety standards and will go into great detail about them. Some hotels have in their guest rooms a special closed-circuit TV channel or brochures to demonstrate the proper safety procedures for fire and other emergencies.

You can find out about fire safety by writing for an excellent booklet available through the National Fire Protection Association (NFPA) and titled *Information on Hotel and Motel Safety for Meeting Planners*. The NFPA is headquartered at Batterymarch Park in Quincy, Massachusetts 02269. Please direct your request to Mr. Albert Sears.

Security

Meeting planners learn a great deal about the seamy side of life when investigating hotel security measures. They also learn a great deal about surveillance and crime deterrence.

Many hotels have installed twenty-four-hour surveillance cameras in lobbies, elevators, and sometimes even the hallways on sleeping-room floors. All hotels should have chains or safety devices on the doors to keep intruders from entering a room even if they have gained possession of a key. Guests should be instructed to keep the chain on at all times when they are in the room.

To inform attendees about security and measures for preventing loss of personal property, many meeting planners include safety and security brochures in the registration confirmation envelope. These forms are sometimes available through the convention and visitors bureau or can be obtained by mail from the professional associations listed in chapter 12.

Facilities for Handicapped Persons

With a housing block of three thousand rooms, many of them double occupancy, it is not unlikely that as many as six or seven thousand people will attend your show. It is possible that a portion of those attendees will have special requirements.

Many organizations for handicapped individuals publish booklets detailing the optimum conditions for their members. Review these publications carefully, and then view all the properties from the vantage point of someone in a wheelchair, with crutches, or with a hearing or sight impairment or from the perspective of a senior citizen. Many hotels set aside rooms with special accommodations for handicapped persons in a wheelchair; such rooms are built with wide doorways, particularly into the bathrooms; high sinks and commodes; easily accessible bathtubs; and wide aisles between bureaus and beds. For the hearing impaired, special flashing lights are installed to alert the person to fire emergencies. Convention staff should be informed of any hearing-or sight-impaired attendees, as well as those who are wheelchair bound, to assist them in case of emergency. The floor housekeeping manager and the security staff should also be apprized of sight-impaired attendees and instructed to clear room-service trays immediately from hallways.

Designating a Headquarters Hotel

If your organization requires that one hotel be designated as headquarters, you will need to supply that hotel with more information than you would provide to other, overflow hotels. Achieving the highly sought after designation of "headquarters hotel" is the goal of all hotel sales managers: Not only will a group block a large number of rooms, but the designation also means additional food-and-beverage income. If you can document that most of your rooms are double occupancy, you will be assuring the hotel of extra income for little effort. Moreover, if you can prove a low no-show factor by producing your last meeting's housing reports, with the added bonus of attracting exhibitors to the hotel, in return for these incentives you should get a good rate for attendees, no charge for meeting rooms, and a liberal complimentary room arrangement.

A Typical Complimentary Room Schedule

The usual number of rooms assigned for complimentary accommodations is one room night for every 50 room nights sold. Assuming a block of 1,400 rooms and an average stay at the hotel of 4 nights, you can anticipate selling 5,600 room nights on peak days, that is, 1,400 times 4. With a 1,400-room block, you should be allowed 28 rooms, each with a 4-day stay, which equals 112 nights, if you are entitled to one night per 50 used (5,600 divided by 50). Therefore, you can house 28 persons at no charge for 4 nights or you can house 14 persons at no charge for 8 nights.

Many meeting planners use these complimentary accommodations for staff housing and for suppliers that would normally charge the organization for accommodations.

Communicating with the Hotels

It is extremely important to be as precise as possible when outlining specific details about your group and its habits. Providing data about expected attendance, room pickup, arrival/departure patterns, and anticipated use of the hotel's food outlets and room service will give the hotel management the necessary information to increase staff during hours of high use and to cut back when the group is away from the hotel.

Staffing for Major Arrivals

A sufficient number of bellhops, registration personnel, and concierge staff must be enlisted if delegates will be arriving by busloads from the airport. Numerous busloads of people, all with a week's worth of luggage, can't be handled by the hotel's usual staff. Additionally, if attendees will be driving to the hotel, valet parking staff should be increased—but this will happen only if the hotel is made aware of your group's habits.

Housekeeping

Included in your instructions to the hotel should be the schedule of the program at the convention center. The hotel will thus get a good idea of when your attendees will be out of the building and can increase staff to have the rooms cleaned by the time everyone returns.

Use of Food Outlets

If the convention center is close to the headquarters and other hotels and attendees are in the habit of lunching at the hotels instead of remaining at the convention center for their meals, the food outlet managers should be informed not only to add staff and even tables but also to order sufficient supplies.

Outside Events

Your headquarters hotel, as well as any other hotel in which you are holding a large block of rooms, should be informed if you will be having a large party away from the area of the hotel on any evening during the show or if an exhibitor is planning an event that will draw a large number of attendees. With this information, the hotels will be able more accurately to assess the staff needed in their lounges and restaurants.

Room Service

When a hotel should staff up for room service can be determined only from your input. In many groups, attendees will have breakfast in their rooms on the first morning and then, after becoming familiar with the neighborhood, will venture out or eat in the hotel coffee shop. You can gauge this information only by communicating with the hotels of last year's show and by closely observing your group's habits.

Making these estimates is never an exact science, but by working together and drawing on the hotel management's experience with groups similar to your own, you will be able to produce a fairly accurate pattern. This attention to detail will save the hotel unnecessary expenses, and you will have saved attendees from undergoing long lines at restaurants and slow service.

Meetings within Meetings: Developing an Efficient
Flow Chart

In my mind, large conventions are like those charming eastern European wooden dolls: Open the doll, and inside there is another doll; open that one, and surprise, another doll appears.

It happens quite often that while a meeting planner is planning a trade show at a convention center he or she is also planning smaller meetings and seminars. And the headquarters hotel is the place where those meetings are usually held.

Communicating with the hotel in an efficient, clear manner about these meetings, as well as about any special events being hosted by the exhibiting association, involves details that are best explained and outlined with a flow chart.

The flow chart below is an example of an easy-to-read and -interpret communication device. Using such a chart in conjunction with flood-and-beverage lists, lists of audiovisual notes and special notes—all cross-referenced on the flow chart and backed up by room diagrams—will greatly facilitate the task of handling the little meetings within the big meeting. And once developed, the plan can be turned over to another staff person for on-site execution.

This chapter has proved one thing: that in order for meeting planners to know their job, they must know everyone else's job. Meeting planners need to understand how a hotel makes money, its day-to-day staff operations, and its management of food-and-beverage outlets. They must know how a housing bureau works and how to organize their housing data to keep the bureau working efficiently. And they must know how to use their exhibitors to enhance their own presence and value to the hotel.

Tuesday, June 2, 1988

Room Name	7:00 a.m.	8:00 a.m.	9:00 a.m.	10:00 a.m.	11:00 a.m.	Noon	1:00 p.m.	2:00 p.m.	3:00 p.m.	4:00 p.m.	5:00 p.m.	6:00 p.m.	8:00 p.m.
Set													
Arizona conf./20	committee 7–9 (breakfast/see f&b chart)		committee 10–noon (coffee service/see f&b chart)					committee 2–5:30 (coffee service see f&b chart)					
New York conf. 35			Board of Directors 9–5 (see food and beverage chart for breakfast, breaks, and lunch info. see AV chart for placement of overhead and screen)									Executive Dinner 6–8:30 (see f&b for dinner info.)	
Missouri theatre/200			Educational Program 9–4:30 (see floor plans for room arrangement, f&b chart for coffee breaks)										
Hawaii classroom/70				Certification Exam 10–3 (see room sets for proper room arrangement and special notes/see f&b chart for refreshments)									
Utah conf. 20		committee 8–10					committee 1–2	committee 2–3					
California conf./20	committee 7–10 (breakfast see f&b chart)					committee lunch 12–1:30 (see f&b chart)				committee 4–5 (coffee service see f&b)			
Mississippi conf./20			committee 9–11				committee 1–3		committee 3:30–5:30				
Oregon hollow sq. 40			National Council 9–5 (see floor plans for special arrangements/f&b for refreshments and lunch/AV chart for proper placement of screens, projectors)										
Maine conf. 15		committee 8–9 (this room can be released after this committee)											

Figure 3–2. *Hotel meeting space flow chart*

4

Evaluating a Convention Center

B ecause a trade show encompasses many activities besides the actual exhibition, the convention center in which it is held must possess sufficient space to house those other activities, as well as adequate service areas to facilitate the move-in, construction, and move-out phases of the event itself. Utilities (such as water and electricity) for operating exhibitor equipment and for the day-to-day functioning of the event must be available and easily accessible. Additional space for meetings, exhibitor and attendee service areas, offices, lounges, storage areas, food outlets, and a registration area are all components of a trade show.

Determining whether or not a convention center has adequate facilities to house a show begins with a site inspection. To simplify that task and to begin with a basis for comparison, assume that your show has a gross-square-footage requirement of 200,000 and that the actual exhibit space, or net-square-footage figure, is 50,000. What takes up the additional 150,000 square feet—that is, what's left after your exhibits are in place? To clearly understand a facility and its relation to a trade show, two phrases need to be defined as they apply to this chapter: net square footage and gross square footage.

Net Square Footage

Net square footage is the real, actual space used for exhibit booths. If a show has sold 150 10-by-10-foot booths, that show has sold exactly 15,000 net square feet of exhibit space. The net square footage is that portion of the space which produces income for the showing organization. Keep in mind that the convention center's final charges to the organization are in part based on the net square footage that has been sold to exhibitors.

Gross Square Footage

The balance of the convention center space is a total of the net square footage (the exhibit space), plus all the other space needed for the show, and this total is the *gross square footage*. It is important to understand how a convention center calculates its gross-square-footage figure in order to gauge how that figure relates to your gross-square-footage needs. The facility's figure could include aisles, pillars, unusable space, dead space for fire lanes and fire doors, food outlets (facility restaurants), meeting rooms, facility management office space, a lobby, and/or any other space not intended for exhibit and meeting use.

A careful analysis of the facility's floor plans and specification sheets is necessary to determine how much of this figure is really available for show purposes.

Planning Gross-Square-Footage Areas

Aisles

An exhibition, when properly planned, should operate like and resemble a city's downtown area. Imagine the exhibits as shops. What links these shops together are the avenues and streets. A great deal of square footage is therefore avenue and street space, or aisles. Aisle space, although a part of the actual exhibit, composes gross square footage.

Food and Other Outlets

To handle the food-and-beverage needs of large groups, food outlets must be built on the exhibit floor and in the public areas of the convention center. Adequate space must be allocated for this use, and the areas that are planned for food outlets constitute a portion of the gross-square-footage figure.

Using Food and Other Outlets Creatively

When considering your gross-square-footage needs and developing a floor plan, think about traffic problem areas and use food and other outlets to remedy any "dead spots"—areas that are less than desirable from an exhibitor's point of view. Typically, the areas near the back of the exhibit hall are not considered ideal for attracting attendees. When you are developing a floor plan, give some thought to the creative placement of outlets to increase traffic through and around the exhibit areas.

Although food and other outlets may appear to be just a service for attendees and exhibitors, they serve a multitude of functions and should be planned as part of your exhibit area floor plan. Properly placed, attractively decorated, and well stocked, such outlets can turn an undesirable piece of exhibit hall real estate into a boon for the small, late, or new exhibitor.

There is no need to limit yourself only to food outlets. Many shows, for example, have successfully created nonprofit boutiques. Museums are particularly well adapted for this approach and make excellent candidates for a boutique area. Contact the public relations departments of local museums and other nonprofit organizations in the city. Well-established environmental groups and charitable organizations with a line of consumer products are other possible candidates.

The displays of books, posters, gift items, jewelry, logo umbrellas, and cards make an attractive addition to a show and give delegates a chance to shop for souvenirs without leaving the show floor. And you can increase exhibitors' chances of making contact with delegates by using these devices to enhance traffic flow and create an inviting atmosphere.

Show Decorator and Audiovisual Contractor Service Booths

Additional gross square footage is consumed by the exhibitors' service booths of the show decorator and the audiovisual contractor. The floor plan below displays the placement of an exhibitors' service booth. During move-in and move-out, exhibitors must employ the services of carpenters, plumbers, electricians, and other workers. The service area becomes the exhibitors' office of operations.

Space for Special Functions

Many organizations hold what is referred to as a plenary session—a fancy name for a meeting at which everyone shows up. Plenary sessions are traditionally held on the opening day of a show and usually are the vehicle for having keynote speakers or the organization's superstars make welcoming remarks and contribute pertinent information about the industry.

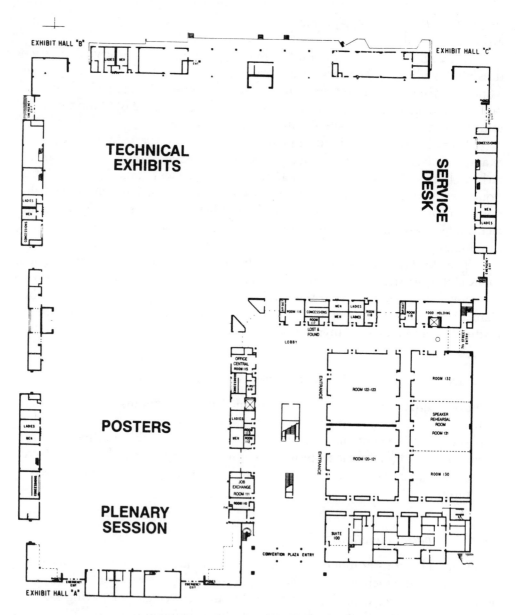

Figure 4–1. *Exhibit hall before booth assignments*

Quite often, a convention center will not have a meeting room or ballroom large enough to hold, all in one place, two to three thousand or more people and extensive audiovisual equipment. In such a case, the meeting planner should set aside a section of the exhibit hall for this use.

Poster Areas

Posters, illuminated view boxes, and booths for technical exhibits are major educational tools at many medical, scientific, and technical shows and are becoming a popular form of disseminating information at nontechnical shows as well. Many shows use these devices exclusively or in conjunction with oral presentations, and they are an integral part of the educational process. Authors of technical papers will sometimes opt for a poster presentation instead of delivering a paper orally, particularly when they (a) are not fluent in the language, (b) suffer from stage fright, or (c) feel that the material is better presented on a poster board, whereby colleagues have time to analyze the information, as opposed to watching quick-changing slides in a ten- to fifteen-minute presentation.

When developing a poster area and calculating square footage, be sure to allow adequate space for aisles. Poster areas attract large numbers of people and are conducive to generating conversation and shoptalk among delegates. Anywhere from a few hundred to several thousand square feet of floor space are typically dedicated to these exhibits; keeping a close watch on the organization's growth will help you estimate total gross-square-footage needs. Meeting rooms have been used for poster displays, and this arrangement is a good alternative if the poster session is not too large. Nonetheless, a well-planned exhibit floor will incorporate adequate space for these presentations and is the preferred solution.

Keeping all poster displays on the exhibit floor will direct traffic flow there and maintain delegate contact with exhibitors. It is not unlikely that the material being viewed in the poster area of an exhibit floor will have been funded by an exhibitor—a relationship that is most obvious at scientific and medical shows.

Lounge Areas

The poster area is an excellent location in which to create a lounge area. Carpeting and high stools also add to the comfort factor when people are viewing technical posters, which are sometimes lengthy and complicated. Creating a comfortable ambience affects the entire mood of a show: This, after all, is what delegates are anticipating when they register for a show—a comfortable environment for learning and for meeting with colleagues.

Storage Areas

At one time, storage of crates and materials was allowed on unused areas of the exhibit floor. The situation is changing, however, because of enhanced fire and safety regulations. If you are permitted some floor space for storage, include that information into your gross-square-footage figures. If you cannot use the exhibit hall for storage space, part of your site inspection should include investigating where empty crates and equipment will be stored during the show.

Quite often you will be allowed to store items in the loading dock area. If not, empty crates will be removed from the facility, stored at a warehouse for the duration of the show, and returned to the convention center for dismantling and move-out.

Ceiling Heights

You will note that the heading above uses the plural—*heights,* not *height.* You would think it an easy task to measure ceiling height, and for almost anyone but a meeting planner that would be true. Get a gigantic ruler, keep extending it until it hits the ceiling, and voilà—ceiling height. True, when the ruler hits the ceiling you have ceiling height, but on its journey upward in an exhibit hall, the ruler passes grids for hanging lights, heating and air-conditioning ducts, flying buttresses leaping out from pillars, architectural oddities, catwalks, and unexpected dropped ceilings in inconvenient places. All this and more will not be evident from a floor plan. If your show has traditionally been a one-story affair and you are faced with the possibility of including two-story exhibits, you must view ceiling height with a cautious eye. Two-story exhibits look like little houses complete with staircases. The extra ceiling height is needed to accommodate not only the structures but the enormous signs that are part of the exhibit, many of them so high that they can be seen from a block away. Large trade shows with similarly large exhibits quite often need a minimum of 25 feet in ceiling height.

Loading Docks and Marshaling Yards

Having an ample number of loading docks is essential for the timely move-in of large shows. Trucks bearing exhibit equipment, carpeting for the exhibit floor, and other materials will be backed up to a loading dock; the materials will then be unloaded from the truck and either driven by forklift or other conveyances to the individual exhibit site outlined on the exhibit floor or taken to other areas of the convention center. The more loading docks that are available, the more trucks that can simultaneously be unloading materials and crates.

While some trucks are unloading goods onto the exhibit floor, others will be waiting in the *marshaling yard*—a large parking area for tractor trailers—for their turn to enter a loading dock. This area can be located either directly outside the loading docks of the convention center or several blocks away.

Timing the Move-in and Move-out Phases

The show decorator, as the coordinator of the move-in procedures, is the person who establishes the move-in and move-out schedule, based on the various types of exhibits in the show. In most cases, the *island exhibits*—that is, unattached structures with aisles on all sides—will be the exhibits that are moved in first. These kinds of exhibits are usually built on the spot, from the ground up, and require the most time to be erected.

Taping the Floor

The actual process of creating an exhibit floor begins just before the truck move-in and commences with taping outlines of the individual configurations on the exhibit floor according to the floor plan. Once the outlines of the individual exhibits have been marked, the actual building of the exhibits begins.

A Typical Move-in Schedule

The following table provides an example of a schedule for island freight delivered to a convention center. In this case, the show is scheduled for an opening day of June 14.

Thursday, June 9 Island booths	1:00 P.M. 19, 30, 31, 32, 33, 35, 36
Friday, June 10 Island booths	8:00 A.M.–12:00 noon 20, 21, 22, 23, 24, 25, 28, 29, 37, 39
Friday, June 10 Island booths	1:00–4:30 P.M. 27, 38
Saturday, June 11 Island booths	1:00–5:00 P.M. 9, 10, 11, 12

By referring to the sample floor plan, you can more easily visualize the island move-in process.

Materials for smaller exhibits and for 10-by-10-foot booths (those created by lining plastic pipe with drapery) are moved in and assembled while the larger booths are being built.

Truck Access onto the Exhibit Floor

Many crates and exhibit materials can be unloaded directly from trucks driven right onto the exhibit floor. Therefore, depending on the number and type of exhibits your show has, the number of *truck entries,* or large runways giving access directly onto the exhibit floor, could be an important factor. If an exhibit hall has ample loading docks and truck entries but access to these areas is poorly planned, timing could be affected. A one-way corridor that allows only one truck at a time to enter or leave could cause major tie-ups during move-in and move-out.

Utilities within the Facility

Utility Outlets

Few shows being produced today need no form of electrical, water, compressed-air, or drainage hookups for their exhibits. Exhibitors need energy to operate machinery, audiovisual equipment, computers, monitors, and anything else that uses energy or produces a waste product. Even a booth set up with a simple living-room environment will need electricity for lamps and other lighting needs. Many of the new convention centers have incorporated electricity, water, gas, compressed air, drains, phone lines, and sometimes even TV satellite hookups into closely spaced floor grids, with additional access to electricity by overhead lines.

Why Exhibitors Need Utilities

Consider the range of shows being produced, the merchandise being displayed therein, and the method of demonstrating these wares and you will quickly see the necessity for adequate energy access and drainage facilities. For example, kitchen appliance shows need sinks, refrigerators, stoves, ovens, and just about everything else you might need in your kitchen, and food companies need the same equipment to prepare food during and to clean up after demonstrations.

Following is a list of associations. Using your imagination, envision what merchandise an exhibitor would display at each type of show, what sources of power and requirements for disposal the exhibitor would have, and what house-keeping problems the exhibitor would encounter during a four-day show.

- In-flight Food Service Association
- Painting and Decorating Contractors of America
- Sealant and Waterproofing Institute
- International Minilab [photographic] Association
- National Dog Groomers Association of America

Given the limitations—because of either size or finances—regarding your site decision, there may not be much you can do about less-than-adequate facilities. You should be aware, however, of the cost to your exhibitors when facilities cannot offer enough power sources.

Plumbing, drain, and gas lines from the source to the booth can, depending on the size of the line (from ½ to 2 inches) cost anywhere from $152 to $225 and up for the first 25 feet, plus $5 to $9 and up for each additional foot—not including labor—to connect the lines. Remember, each gas, drain, and water line is a separate installation and does not include the cost of the utility, that is, the cost of gas, electricity, and so on.

Electrical costs depend on the number of outlets installed and anticipated wattage use. A single outlet for up to 3,000 watts could run as high as $200; a floodlight for 500 watts, $150; power-motor outlets for a 2-horsepower engine, $165. None of these figures include labor for installation or removal.

Rules and Regulations

Fire and Building Codes

Individual cities will, naturally, have their own rules and regulations regarding fire and public safety. On major safety points, however, there is little variation.

Fire and Safety Management. Fire and safety management is under the jurisdiction of the facility's fire marshal, who is responsible for enforcing all public and fire safety laws. The fire marshal will provide guidance for you and the show decorator regarding preparation of your floor plan. This official has responsibility for reviewing booth layouts and construction; for monitoring the show, from move-in through move-out, for violations; for overseeing the interior decorations, furnishings, and finishes of the exhibits and determining whether they meet all code requirements; for authorizing and controlling use of any restricted materials; and for making a final inspection before the show opens.

City Building Codes. Many cities require that a licensed engineer safety-certify all exhibits for structural soundness before the plans are submitted to the convention center for approval.

Fire and Building Safety Approval of Exhibits. After exhibits are approved by a licensed engineer, the convention center management and the individual meeting planner must ensure that plans for all exhibits adhere to show rules regarding fire safety and structural soundness. Additional approval may be needed for two-story structures, booths with canopies, platforms whose area exceeds 500 square feet, covered booths, and any structures more than 12 feet high.

An excellent overview of an individual facility's guidelines regarding fire safety and building codes is found in the National Association of Exhibit Managers' (NAEM) *Annual Guide to Exposition Services* (see the list of suggested readings at the back of this book). This guide contains helpful information about individual facilities' building and fire codes, as well as guidelines on labor unions.

The Exhibitor Service Kit

Exhibitor service kits are developed by the meeting planner to inform all exhibiting companies about the rules and regulations for fire and safety. These kits also include forms for ordering utilities (water, compressed air, gas, electricity, telephones), services (booth cleaning, food-and-beverage services, audiovisual equipment, flowers, furniture), and anything else an exhibitor may need to create a booth. Also included in the kit are (a) labor rates for the various tradespeople needed to install and dismantle an exhibit and (b) labor union rules and regulations.

In addition to the above information, which pertains directly to the exhibition aspect of a trade show, an assessment of the nonexhibit areas of the building must be made as they relate to the educational program and other service areas of a convention.

Convention Center Facilities

Accommodations for Disabled Persons and Senior Citizens

For meeting the needs of special populations, meeting planners should carefully review all the material available on the convention center. Most older centers have updated and modernized their facilities to accommodate the needs of disabled persons and the elderly, but you should ascertain, for yourself and in the framework of your show and delegates, what is needed and what is available.

Telephones. The center should have an adequate number of low-placed phones in all areas for easy access by people using wheelchairs, by children, or by anyone else who would have difficulty reaching the coin slot and buttons on standard telephone company equipment. Those unable to reach a standard telephone should not have to hunt for a phone they can use, nor should they have to ask strangers for assistance.

Bathrooms. All bathrooms should have wide doorways for easy access, as well as specially outfitted toilet facilities. Stalls should be equipped with special commodes and handrails; a mirror, a sink, and soap and towel dispensers should be within reach. Doors to individual stalls should swing inward and be at least 32 inches wide. And whereas the men's room should have at least one urinal that is no more than 19 inches high, any feminine-hygiene-product dispensers in the women's room should be low enough for easy access. Ramps should be available wherever there are changes in floor levels.

Main Entrance. A curbside should be cut for access to wheelchairs. Ramps should be available if the entrance is not at street level. All doorways, corridors, and aisles should be at least 32 inches wide to accommodate wheelchairs.

Water Fountains. A sufficient number of easily accessible water fountains should be available throughout the center.

Elevators. Elevators should have a door opening of at least 32 inches, with a minimum interior to 60 by 60 inches for easy wheelchair turnaround. The top button on the controls should be no more than 48 inches from the floor, and the controls should contain braille symbols. Audible floor announcements are a nice amenity for those with sight impairments, and all floor indicators should be large and bright enough to be easily read.[1]

Floors. Nonskid floor surfaces are a definite plus. If they are not available, they may have to be laid in the public areas if your show attracts a large number of disabled or elderly delegates.

Meeting Rooms. If the convention offers educational programs, meeting rooms for seminars will most likely be set up in a theater-style configuration. Leave space for wheelchairs so that they will neither block the aisles nor make the persons in wheelchairs stand out in the crowd.

Facilities for Seeing-Eye Dogs. Some shows attract a large number of sight-impaired delegates; others, only a few. If any delegates are accompanied by a seeing-eye dog, make sure there are enough safe areas for the dogs to be walked. Fresh water and a feeding area should be arranged well in advance of the show.

General Specifications for the Center

Public Rest Rooms. The facility should have an adequate number of rest rooms on the exhibit floor and on the meeting-room floors, with signs pointing the way. Some shows attract a larger contingent of one sex than of the other. To alleviate long lines at the rest rooms when there is a preponderance of one sex— say, 75 percent—have the convention center change the signs so that 75 percent of the rest rooms will accommodate that sex.

Meeting Rooms. Convention centers can never seem to keep up with the demand for meeting rooms. More and more organizations, particularly medical associations, offer educational programs. Quite often these programs are the primary reason for attending the convention: Continuing education credits for medical subjects can be obtained only through attending educational seminars, such education-intensive programs offering as much as thirty hours of continuing education credit.

Flexibility of Meeting-Room Space. Although the number of meeting rooms is a significant factor in determining the suitability of a site, of equal importance are the capacity specifications and the range of capacities of the meeting rooms. Flexibility of space is also a consideration. Rooms that can be altered to change size by the addition or removal of air walls greatly enhance a site's desirability.

Meeting-Room Ceiling Height. Many educational programs begin with an opening session that attracts a large number of delegates. A room capable of holding thousands of people is necessary, but the session is usually a onetime event. A room with a seating capacity of three to four thousand subsequently divided into three rooms seating from one to fifteen hundred persons apiece is an ideal setup. The room, opened to full capacity (that is, for three thousand people) should have ceilings high enough to accommodate the audiovisual equipment needed for a group of that size—that is, ceilings high enough to accommodate one or more screens 18 feet square, with staging for the speakers raised at a level high enough to be seen by everyone in the room. The audiovisual supervisor will construct a plan to set up the room for the onetime large session in such a way that the maintenance and audiovisual crews have only to pull the air walls, rearrange a few rows of chairs, and make final adjustments to the projectors in order to create individual meeting rooms that can be used immediately after the opening session. This situation is quite common and, when properly planned and orchestrated, can be dealt with in about thirty minutes. Naturally, it takes the concerted effort of everyone involved—the convention center's laborers, your audiovisual staff, and most of all, your final speaker.

Allocation of Meeting Space. Some topics, those of a more general nature, will naturally attract greater numbers of delegates than more esoteric topics will. Therefore, smaller rooms are needed to accommodate these seminars. The only way to make decisions on the allocation of meeting-room space is through accurate record keeping and actual head counts.

Why Proper Room Allocations Are Important. Why all the concern with allocating the right session to the proper room? Budget and comfort. Naturally, you want to know what topics attract the largest crowds so that you can properly accommodate them in the largest rooms. But examining past attendance records and carefully analyzing your program before establishing your meeting-room usage will save money as well. You will not be setting up more rooms than you need, and you will be using more efficiently all the rooms you have set up. With meeting rooms at a premium and audiovisual costs for equipment and labor a high-priced item, you can't be too detailed in analyzing your meeting-room needs.

Thirty to forty rooms, in a range of sizes, are not too many. A program that runs for four to five days could hold as many as nine or more simultaneous sessions; therefore the educational program alone would use nine or more meeting rooms.

The following list of ancillary room allocations will give you further information on room needs in addition to those for meeting rooms.

Number of Rooms	Use
2	Press
1 (large, lockable)	Audiovisual equipment storage (microphones, monitors, and any other portable equipment)
1 (large)	Show communications office
1 (large, lockable)	Accounting
1 (large, lockable)	Equipment storage for program videotaping (sometimes a company other than your audiovisual company) cameras, lenses, and so on
1 (large, lockable)	Show manager's office
1 (large, lockable)	Exhibitors' lounge
1 set up conference style for maximum attendance	Staff meeting room
3 set up conference style for 10 to 20 persons apiece	Swing space for ad hoc or last-minute meetings
3 set up theater style for various sizes	Affiliated group programs
3 not set up	Space for special food functions, receptions, and so on
1 (lockable)	Staff storage for personal items, supplies, and so on
1 (large, lockable)	Speaker rehearsal room

Together with the nine meeting rooms for the educational program, a total of twenty-nine rooms must be available for the show.

Lighting. Some older facilities do not offer a great deal of flexibility in lighting range. The range of lighting for your needs may not be available, the meeting room being equipped with merely an on/off switch or a rheostat that reduces the light in the entire room. When a room is divided, the lighting should be individualized for each section. (I have seen facilities where one section required darkness, and when the lights were turned off two or three other rooms were put into darkness at the same time.) Also important is having flexibility within the room; depending on where you set your screens, the lights directly over them will have to be disconnected, by hand, if individual lighting controls have not been built into the room.

Task Lighting. Sometimes it is necessary for meeting planners, when faced with unsophisticated lighting controls, to add lighting to rooms. If all you can do is have the lights on or off, you will need to install *task lighting*—that is, special lighting designed to enable people to take notes and walk safely during sessions when the lights are out.

Room Accessories and Equipment

Sign Easels

Sign easels may sound like an insignificant item, but if the convention center does not have an ample supply of them, it could be expensive to have to rent easels from your show decorator.

The easel inventory in convention centers could range from twenty to two hundred. Find out how many easels are in stock, how many are in good repair, and what they look like. Most convention centers offer easels for no charge, but it's best to check.

Staging

Staging, sometimes referred to as risers, is usually required in large meeting rooms that will be set up for several hundreds or thousands of people. It is on the staging that head tables or a speaker's dais will be placed; the staging serves to elevate an event's speakers and make them visible to people seated at the back of the room. The capacity of the room will determine the height of the risers. Many convention centers offer staging, with setup fees included in the cost of renting the center. As with easels, check on the inventory and condition of the staging.

Skirting

The bottom of a stage is not attractive; indeed, it detracts from the appearance of a meeting room. Tables on the staging are designed for function, not appearance. In both cases, skirting is needed to mask the unattractive features of this furniture. Tables in particular need skirting, since there is something comical about a row of human legs, shins bared, wrapped around the legs of chairs or in whatever other unsightly position people usually put their legs into when sitting at a table. To preserve the modesty of female speakers and to keep those persons in pants looking like adults, skirt your tables.

The rules for skirts are the same as for easels. Convention centers sometimes have skirting material in stock and do not charge for their use; other times, they do charge. Either way, ask to see the material. You may be unhappy with the colors and opt to have the show decorator supply the skirting. If the skirting supplied by the convention center is in a useful, visually undisturbing color but you are not going to be using the hall for another four or five years, find out how often the center replaces the material and whether such replacement will occur just before or just after you are expected in town.

Air-Conditioning and Heating

Trade shows and conventions are held during all seasons and in all parts of the world. Sometimes it's hot, sometimes it's cold, and sometimes—though not often—the weather is just right. Although during the show you will be supplied with heat and power or air-conditioning and power, the times when the heat or air-conditioning will be turned on should be clearly spelled out in the contract.

In particular, you must make sure that the contract clearly states the rates for heat or air-conditioning during move-in and move-out. These dates are not a part of your show dates, and therefore such costs may be not a part of the rental costs but an added expense—a point that meeting planners sometimes overlook. If a show is in the North during the fall or winter months, it is not unlikely that you will be experiencing harsh weather. You will also be experiencing harsh looks from the crew if you cannot afford to heat (or, conversely, cool) the hall during move-in. If you want to heat or cool the center during these moving days, ask the convention services manager of the facility to give you a cost estimate.

Setup Charges

Many halls allow a onetime setup of meeting rooms without charge; after that, any room-setup changes are charged to your account. Depending on the city and the facility, unplanned room changes could be costly.

Creating a Flow Chart of the Show's Program

Planning ahead with careful attention to the program not only will make a difference in the show's economic picture but also will manifest itself positively when you are on-site. Careless planning, by contrast, can put a burden on the labor crew and create an atmosphere of confusion that affects the mental health of your own staff members when they feel that no one is in control.

Developing a flow chart to track meeting-room use and to focus on the hour-by-hour use of the entire facility will eliminate last-minute changes in room setups and give the convention services manager a comprehensive overview of the entire convention.

The flow chart in figure 4–2 includes a great deal of information. It represents one day of activities for a five-day meeting. The information covered includes the following: rooms used, square footage of each room, number of chairs needed for each room, time of use, break times, lunch time, special set-up notations, and information on any changes for the next day's program

Using the Flow Chart to Allocate Labor

The flow chart is, as noted, the best means for communicating your instructions to the convention services manager of the facility. It also serves another, equally important purpose: Since the convention services manager will know well in advance the number and type of employees he or she must enlist for every aspect of your show, from move-in to move-out, by efficiently planning this individual's labor needs for your show you will save on excessive labor costs.

Timing Housekeeping Services during the Show

By referring to the flow chart, the convention services manager will clearly see overall daily time allocations—that is, precisely when the show opens, breaks for coffee and for lunch, and ends its program for the day. Depending on the number of food outlets erected in the exhibit hall and in the public areas of the center's lobby and corridors, the convention services manager will be able to see when the heaviest use of these outlets will occur and when to increase staff for cleaning. Table busing is crucial to the overall appearance of the show: If there is not enough labor, things can get pretty messy.

Room	120/1/4/5	123/7	130–132	260/4	261	263/7	264	270	271	274	275
Sq. Ft.	7,740	5,040	12,768	5,040	1,350	5,040	2,520	1,200	1,200	4,256	4,256
Set Theatre	800	500	1,100	500	135	500	250	125	125	400	400
8:30–10:00	session 1	session 2	session 3	not in use	session 4	session 5	no tech.	session 6	session 7	not in use	not in use
10:00–10:30	BREAK	BREAK	BREAK	BREAK	BREAK	BREAK	BREAK	BREAK	BREAK	BREAK	BREAK
10:30–12:00	session 8	not in use	session 9	session 10	not in use	session 11	not in use	not in use	session 12 (overhead)	not in use	session 13
12:00–1:30	LUNCH	LUNCH	LUNCH	LUNCH	LUNCH	LUNCH	LUNCH	LUNCH	LUNCH	LUNCH	LUNCH
1:30–3:00	session 14	session 15	session 16	not in use	session 17	session 18	not in use	not in use	not in use	session 19	session 20
3:00–3:30	BREAK	BREAK	BREAK	BREAK	BREAK	BREAK	BREAK	BREAK	BREAK	BREAK	BREAK
3:30–5:00	not in use	not in use	session 21	session 22	session 23	session 24	session 25	reset schoolroom for a.m. session	session 26	not in use	session 27

Figure 4–2. *Flow chart for convention center meetings*

Other Uses for the Flow Chart

In addition to its use for allocating service and room-setup labor and equipment for the show, the flow chart can also be used to allocate audiovisual labor for the meeting rooms. A more detailed discussion of staging audiovisual move-in can be found in chapter 10.

General Site Information

Damage Liability

It is customary for the convention services manager, the meeting planner, and the show decorator to conduct a walk-through just prior to move-in. Armed with a pad and pencil and, if necessary, a camera, make notes on your floor plan of any existing damage to the structure, any heavily soiled areas, and any rips or tears in wall coverings. After move-out, the same tour will be conducted to determine what, if any, damage occurred during your occupancy of the building. If there is significant damage, the showing organization is liable for the cost of repair. Thus, making accurate notes during the initial walk-through is important, should there be a question of liability.

Many convention centers charge for excessive trash removal and for removing residue from tape on the exhibit floor. The tape residue occurs from the initial outlining of the booths. If the cleaning staff has to remove the tape residue, the organization renting the hall will be charged accordingly.

Traffic, Rock Concerts, Ball Games, Parades, Local
Celebrations, and Other Events

Even the most well engineered and planned exhibit hall can, during move-in, be held hostage by local traffic. Although you can't stop the traffic, knowledge of the rush-hour patterns and the streets and avenues trucks will use to gain access to the hall from the major highway exits must be considered when planning your move-in and -out schedule.

If you are booking a facility for a citywide convention, you will most likely be looking at a date at least three and probably five or seven years in advance. Although it is impossible to predict sporting-event schedules, if the city of your choice boasts a team in any of the popular sports and your show is being planned when that sport is in season, you should be aware of the sports arena's proximity to the convention center. If access to the convention center is off a highway exit that serves as access to the arena, you could have a logistics problem with trucks during move-in and move-out.

Local parades, fairs, rock concerts, and so on are usually listed in city calendars. If a local annual event is held on the third Saturday in June and that's your move-in time, you may have to arrange for an evening move-in. You can get help from and most likely will be offered assistance by the local police. If you have some flexibility in scheduling, check the highway system to determine which exits the trucks are likely to use. Follow the route they will be advised or compelled to take, and map out a plan with the show decorator, rescheduling or adjusting move-in and -out time as appropriate.

Shuttle-Bus Access

Ideally, the exhibit hall should have either an entire block available for shuttle-bus pickup and drop-off or a special loading and unloading area off the street and away from local traffic. Large groups whose hotels are not within walking distance will require ample space for shuttle buses during peak hours. The logistical problems of shuttle systems, including the number of buses needed and their routing, are covered in chapter 11. Even with a small show, however, you could have as many as five or six buses lined up outside the convention center's main entrance. Loading and unloading passengers takes time, and despite a dispatcher's best efforts and clear, uncomplicated signs, there is inevitably the errant delegate jumping off one bus and onto another. And because inclement weather can make things uncomfortable for delegates too, the existence of overhangs protecting the sidewalk from rain and snow is definitely a plus.

At this point, you have looked at the convention center inside and out and from the perspective of exhibitors, audiovisual technicians, tradespeople, and delegates. Remember that not all of the desirable features outlined are likely to be in one convention center, that most problems are solvable, and that the objective is to maximize the former and minimize the latter.

5
Creating a Trade Show

Two hundred thousand square feet of exhibit space. Two hundred thousand square feet of *empty* exhibit space. For first-time users of an exhibit hall, nothing is quite so intimidating as walking through an empty exhibit hall—or worse, an empty exhibit hall with just a few tractor trailers scattered around for perspective—with the knowledge that it is your job to fill all that space, as well as the entire convention center, including the meeting rooms, the lobby, and the lounge areas.

The Show Decorator

All supplier companies that you have contracted with—the audiovisual company, ground operators, security firms, hotels, registration personnel, entertainers, and the show decorator—become, in essence, temporary employees of the association.

With the exception of the show decorator, all these contractors work with the meeting planner for the twelve or eighteen months it takes to plan a convention in a city, and many of the suppliers are drawn from the convention city. I say "with the exception of the show decorator" because it is this supplier that is more closely involved with the show. Few meeting planners responsible for large conventions change show decorators from year to year. Destination management companies, by the nature of their work—that is, functioning as your link to the city's resources for entertainment, intracity transportation, and the myriad other things needed during a convention, such as printing, airport greeters, and coordination of special events—rarely "follow the show." With show decorators, however, the involvement with members of the organization and its exhibitors is more complex and this supplier usually enjoys a multiyear contract.

Responsibilities of the Show Decorator

The show decorator's responsibilities are the following:

- Overseeing the actual development of the exhibit hall

- Organizing the move-in, building, and move-out phases of the show in a timely manner

- All show decorating, including drapes, signs, the registration area, and aisle carpeting in the exhibit hall and elsewhere as needed; creating concession food-stand areas; and supplying equipment and furniture where needed

- Hiring all labor to facilitate the installation and dismantling of the entire show

The show decorator typically works with the meeting planner well in advance of the actual move-in and, if the facility is new to both decorator and planner, will often accompany the meeting planner on a site inspection.

Decorator Experience

An experienced show decorator is a valuable asset to a meeting planner, since that person has worked in many halls and cities and understands the advantages and drawbacks of each site. If, for instance, a hall is adequate but access to the city and to the convention center is difficult for the large trucks needed for many shows, it will be the show decorator's knowledge and experience that will alert the meeting planner to this situation so that plans can be made to deal with the problem. It is also the show decorator who is wise to the ways of the labor force in various cities and who possesses up-to-date information on those union rules and regulations in each jurisdiction which could affect on-site management.

Choosing a Show Decorator

Obviously, choosing a good show decorator is key to a show's look and overall success. The way to make that choice is to arm yourself, before contracts are signed, with as much knowledge as possible about the various show decorators. There are basically two ways to acquire this information. The first, more informal method is to obtain word-of-mouth recommendations (or criticisms) from fellow meeting planners—in short, trade gossip. The second method is to gather information from the show-decorating companies themselves. After you have settled on a few real candidates, ask for a written proposal. This document should include a list of services with a brief description of each item, the price per item, and a total price.

Since the proposal will be based on information you supply, it is important that you outline in a request for a proposal all the elements of the show.

Sending a Request for a Proposal to a Show Decorator

The information needed for a show decorator to accurately assess a show and in turn develop a proposal should include specifications for the following:

- Registration area plan and furnishings
- Meeting rooms
- Signage
- Exhibit floor, entranceways, and lounge areas
- Booths
- Suggested lighting, floral/greenery arrangements, banners, and carpeting
- Any special concerns or requirements unique to your particular show
- Furniture for show offices
- Freight handling for the association and exhibitors
- Labor use for installation and dismantling, based on the previous show

A Typical Proposal

The information below, from a decorator's proposal, will help you to understand some of the elements involved in such a document. Although perhaps initially overwhelming, a good proposal should outline the entire event, broken down into sections. Handled this way, a proposal's creativity and cost can easily be assessed.[1]

Convention Center Entrance

As the buses pull into the drive, your attendees will be met with a 10-foot-high by 40-foot-long banner. The banner will cost approximately $2,400. This banner will be installed against the concrete facing above the main entrance to the convention center and will read:

> **WELCOME**
> **SOCIETY OF TREE SURGEONS**
> **NINETY-NINTH ANNUAL MEETING**

Registration and Meeting Rooms

The background to the registration area will be draped, floor to ceiling, in a combination of red, white, and blue. Suspended on the backdrape will be a banner welcoming your attendees and indicating show hours.

As an alternative to using draped, counter-high tables for sign-in, modular counters will be provided. These counters will be color coordinated and are well suited to adding informational and instructional signs.

For directional purposes, we will provide ten mounted floor plans for the meeting rooms. These plans will be distributed throughout the meeting-room area. Each plan will have a "You are Here" arrow attached to it for quick-and-easy reference by attendees.

Suspended over the south entrance to the meeting rooms will be a sign indicating access to meeting rooms 1–17. This sign will be double-sided, with the reverse side directing people to the north and south exhibit entrances. Chaser lights will run around the entire perimeter, drawing further attention to the sign. (Chaser lights are lights that flash in a sequential pattern or "chase" each other around a display.)

Suspended over the north entrance will be a sign indicating meeting rooms 18–28, 30–32, 29–31, and 33–37. Arrows will further designate appropriate directions. Again, the reverse side of the sign will direct people to the north and south exhibit entrances. This sign will also be provided with a circumference of chaser lights.

All signage will be color coordinated for the show. Any signs pertaining to the meeting rooms will be done in red and white; any signs pertaining to the exhibit hall will be done in blue and white. Registration and meeting rooms will cost $1,980.

Entrance Unit

The hallway between the plenary room and the exhibit hall is approximately 20 feet wide. We propose a modular entranceway approximately 12 feet tall, spanning the hallway, which cuts the opening down to 10 feet in width. Complementing this unit will be floral/greenery arrangements. The support panels will be utilized to indicate show hours, information concerning the scientific area, or other information you wish included. The reverse side of the unit could indicate the future meetings and dates.

Because of the flexibility of this particular unit, you may also consider eliminating the inside columns. We would then fill in these areas with tall trees surrounded by smaller floral/greenery arrangements. As you can see from the enclosed photographs, we can interchange panels in show colors and incorporate the show logo as well. Cost of entranceway: $1,200.

The above information is merely to illustrate the detail that a good show decorator will put into a proposal. Other points included in this particular proposal were the following:

- Floor plans
- Poster sessions
- Furniture
- Aisle signs in the exhibit hall
- Aisle carpeting
- Restaurant/theme center
- Freight handling
- Exhibitor services
- Labor for installation and dismantling
- Electrical services
- Personnel
- Exhibitor pricing and credit policy

Evaluating the Proposals

When all the proposals are in, read them carefully for signs of an imagination at work—or of the opposite, a drone who sees your show as just another job. Sometimes it pays to go with the more creative firm, even if that company appears more costly on the surface. Such a firm may also be more imaginative in helping you stay within budgetary guidelines.

Union Relationships

As stated earlier in this chapter, the show decorator is responsible for hiring labor for a show. He or she is responsible not only for seeing that sufficient labor is available during the installation and dismantling of exhibits but also for contracting for that labor. Consequently, the show decorator is also responsible for relations with the labor unions in the particular city.

The complexities of staging a trade show, by nature a highly labor-intensive affair, are at times overwhelming. Add to these complexities the variables of state laws and union jurisdictions and the first-time convention manager might well feel discouraged. Moreover, given that many convention centers and cities are booked several years in advance, it is hardly possible to foresee what situations might affect the labor pool for your show. Only by understanding unions and their jurisdictions, rules, and regulations will you be able to deal with them in the most professional manner.

Educating Exhibitors about Union Regulations

It is the responsibility of the convention manager and the show decorator to educate exhibitors as to individual city and state regulations regarding unions. When problems arise, they are usually caused by miscommunication or misunderstanding.

Included in the exhibitor service kit should be labor order forms for the installation and dismantling of booths, electrical and water lines, and any other necessary items, along with a listing of standard and overtime rates and when each rate is in effect (that is, hours and days of the week). Accompanying this practical information should be the rules and regulations concerning labor and proper protocol when dealing with union labor.

Union Jurisdictions

Unions that are most commonly used and have jurisdiction over trade shows vary from city to city but typically include the following:

- *Carpenters.* In charge of the construction of most things wooden—framework, windows, doors, paneling, cabinets, and so on. They are also responsible for building exhibit booths and, depending on the city, may also be allowed to lay carpets. In some places, there are subspecialities, such as rough-work carpentry and finish carpentry.

- *Electrical workers.* Plan and assemble electrical equipment—wiring for lighting and for running exhibitor equipment like stoves, refrigerators, and medical apparatus.

- *General labor.* Manual laborers without formal training in any specific skill like carpentry or electrical work. General labor is hired to handle freight but normally is not allowed to operate machinery.

- *Ironworkers/riggers.* Responsible for erecting beams, frameworks for signs, and other parts of an exhibit that uses metal. They are usually employed to set up the stairways inside two-story booths.

- *Millwrights.* Millwrights build wooden platforms used for the display of equipment. They are also allowed to work with and dismantle the equipment, using various hand and power tools.

- *Operating engineers.* Operate forklifts, cranes, and other construction equipment.

- *Painters.* Allowed to paint interiors and exteriors.

- *Plumbers and pipe fitters.* Responsible for installing pipes.

- *Stagehands.* Handle scenery, props, and stage equipment and operate and dismantle audiovisual equipment.

- *Audiovisual technicians.* Set up rooms with audiovisual equipment, manage projection equipment during sessions, and adjust lighting.

- *Teamsters.* Responsible for driving trucks.

- *Union business agent.* An official who is *elected* by the unions and whose responsibility is to find work for union members.

- *Shop steward.* An on-site representative who ensures that the rights of workers from his or her union are being protected and that laborers are working in a safe and healthy environment.

- *Shop fore-person.* Also sees to the rights of workers and the working environment.

These areas of labor jurisdiction are the most commonly used during a trade show. The tasks vary from city to city, convention center to convention center, and jurisdiction to jurisdiction; they also depend on the amount of available labor in each city.

Awareness Programs for Labor Unions

Many city governments, aware of the economic advantages that trade shows offer to a city, are instituting awareness programs with the labor unions. Sensitivity sessions have also been introduced to help union workers understand the problems that exhibitors and show managers face when putting on a trade show. Such programs explain to workers that a trade show means clean, safe work and, with the union's cooperation, regular work in a labor force that is often beset by unemployment. Keeping a city booked with trade shows means keeping the labor force employed. Since a decision by a meeting planner to show or not show is quite often based on a city's reputation for service and labor relations, it is to the unions' own benefit to understand the role such shows play in the economic health of their city.

Right-to-Work States

The phrase *right to work* is applied to individual states that have a right-to-work law in effect. Such a law allows—but limits exhibiting companies to bring in their own labor to set up and dismantle exhibits. The limits usually specify that such workers be full-time employees of the exhibiting company. Your show decorator is the person to consult on a specific state's right-to-work policies.

Food Service

Many meeting planners make arrangements to open food-service stands throughout the convention center during the move-in, as a courtesy to workers and especially if the convention center is located in an area that lacks a large selection of eating establishments.

Figure 5–1 depicts the food-service schedule for an entire show as it relates to public food distribution, beginning with the move-in, continuing through the show to service attendees, and following through the move-out. The actual show dates in this example are June 14–17; move-in occurs June 9–13. The schedule outlines anticipated head counts for laborers' food requirements during move-in and gradually escalates to a full day in which attendees frequent all the food outlets.

Budget

A financial picture of a trade show will reduce to line items the various costs to the convention manager of on-site show interior decoration. The figures given below are based on 1988 average costs. The example represents the costs of basic decorations and furnishings, as well as of the labor needed to install and dismantle the equipment and furnishings.

Rental

116 10-by-10-foot pipe-and-drape booths @ $20.00	$ 2,320
32 island exhibits, marked and taped @ $26.00	832
7 draped writing tables in registration area @ $33.00	231

Food Service Schedule
(June 14–17, 1988)

Area	Fri 6/10	Sat 6/11	Sun 6/12	Mon 6/13	Tues 6/14	Wed 6/15	Thurs 6/16	Fri 6/17	Sat 6/18
1 Exhibit hall A					10 a.m. 5 p.m.	10 a.m. 5 p.m.	10 a.m. 5 p.m.	8:30 a.m. 5 p.m.	8 a.m. 3 p.m.
2 Exhibit hall B					10 a.m. 5 p.m.	10 a.m. 5 p.m.	10 a.m. 5 p.m.	8:30 a.m. 5 p.m.	
3 Exhibit hall C			8 a.m. 5 p.m.	7 a.m. 7 p.m.	10 a.m. 5 p.m.	10 a.m. 5 p.m.	10 a.m. 5 p.m.	8:30 a.m. 5 p.m.	
4 Exhibit hall C		8 a.m. 5 p.m.	8 a.m. 5 p.m.	7 a.m. 7 p.m.	10 a.m. 5 p.m.	10 a.m. 5 p.m.	10 a.m. 5 p.m.	8:30 a.m. 5 p.m.	
5 Deli Exhibit hall					10 a.m. 5 p.m.	10 a.m. 5 p.m.	10 a.m. 5 p.m.	8:30 a.m. 5 p.m.	
6 Mezzanine				7 a.m. 3 p.m.	7 a.m. 5 p.m.	7 a.m. 5 p.m.	7 a.m. 5 p.m.	7 a.m. 5 p.m.	
7 Mezzanine				7 a.m. 3 p.m.	7 a.m. 5 p.m.	7 a.m. 5 p.m.	7 a.m. 5 p.m.	7 a.m. 5 p.m.	
Estimated headcount	50	100	400	1800	2000	2500	2000	500	100

Figure 5–1. *Food service schedule*

Miscellaneous draping around hall: 1,700 feet @ $1.50 per foot	2,550
Message center table and stand	35
250 4-by-8-foot poster boards @ $37.00	9,250
7,388 yards of aisle carpeting including installation, removal, and daily cleaning, @ $4.50 per yard	33,246
70 stools for poster area @ $25.00	1,750
2 entrance units @ $1,320	2,640
30 55-gallon trash containers @ $25.00	750

Painting and printing of signs:

43 22-by-28-inch signs @ $63.00	$ 2,709
60 11-by-14-inch signs @ $21.00	1,260
6 28-by-44-inch signs @ $154.00	924
495 4-by-4-inch signs @ $1.60	792
11 7-by-44-inch signs @ $25.00	275
Total rental costs	$59,564

Labor

Set up and remove poster boards

50 man-hours × $60.00 per hour	$3,000
10 man-hours × 30.00 per hour	300

Set up and remove signs and banners

17 man-hours × $60.00 per hour	1,020
10 man-hours × 30.00 per hour	300

Special decorations (lounge areas and restaurants)

22 man-hours × $60.00 per hour	1,320

Miscellaneous labor (move boxes, open and shut drapes to control traffic flow, set out meeting-room signs)

10 man-hours × $60.00 per hour	600
6 man-hours × $30.00 per hour	180

Set up and remove entrance units

14 man-hours × $60.00 per hour	840
4 man-hours × $30.00 per hour	120

Summary
   113 overtime hours @ $60.00 per hour $6,780
   30 standard-time hours @ $30.00 per hour   900

Total labor $7,680

Selling the Show

Developing an Exhibitor Prospectus

An *exhibitor prospectus* is the first communication between a convention manager and potential exhibitors. An exhibitor prospectus has many aspects and
usually appears as a multipage brochure presenting all the facts that an exhibitor,
actual or potential, needs to buy space at your show. A typical prospectus could
include the following:

- Expected attendance at the convention

- Attendee profile

- Cancellation rebate policy

- Cost per square foot of exhibit space

- Labor information and rates

- Move-in/move-out schedule

- Display rules and regulations

- Exhibitor housing information

- Exhibitor registration information

- List of previous exhibitors

- Fire and safety regulations

- Pertinent statistical information (for example: "Last year, your automobile show had sixty thousand attendees, eleven thousand serious inquiries,
  and three thousand automobile sales)

- Security information

- Service contractor or show decorator information

- Services included in the cost of exhibit space

- Show colors

- Show dates

- Show location

- Description of a standard booth

- Terms and conditions of the contract

- Preliminary floor plan

Allocating Exhibit Space

The position of each exhibitor on the exhibit floor can be determined by several methods. Some shows use a lottery system; others, a first-come, first-served arrangement.

Many shows base requests for position on the exhibit floor on a *point priority system*—a system that gives the meeting planner complete control over the appearance of the show and that, although complicated, ensures fairness in allocating space to all exhibitors, large or small. The detailing below of a typical point priority system will answer many of the questions that aspiring show managers have about how a floor plan is developed.

A Typical Point Priority System (excerpted from an actual Exhibitor Prospectus of The Society of Nuclear Medicine)

One point will be allowed for every 100 square feet taken at last year's exhibit and one point for every continuous year exhibited over the past five years. In addition, five bonus points will be given to those companies whose applications are received before the deadline.

In addition to the above factors, the date of receipt of the first application will initiate a thirty-day priority assignment period. (A handicap system using the most distant mailing point will be employed so that no geographical location has an undue advantage.) All applications will be dated upon receipt. Those applications received on the first day or on the following four days will each receive an additional five points. One point will be subtracted from the five-point maximum for applications received each five-day period thereafter. No points in this category will be given for applications received after the thirty-day period.

Applications received from companies that have merged with, have been purchased by, or have purchased companies will receive those priority points which have been earned by the company with the most favorable exhibit history—not the total of both companies' points.

The floor plan included in the prospectus is proposed as indicated. After receipt of the application for exhibit space by (date), the revised floor plan will be drawn up and sent to all exhibitors. At that time, if there is conflict between or among exhibitors, the amount of advertising taken in the association's magazine will be used to break ties and settle disputes.

Reviewing Exhibitors' Floor Plans

Most organizations require that exhibitors send a complete floor plan of their booths, giving all dimensions for height, depth, and construction material. The plans are then reviewed for compliance with the rules of the show and the facility.

Many shows allow booths to be built to the very edge of their space. This arrangement allows the exhibitors more exhibiting area but gives a dense, crowded appearance to the exhibit floor. Other shows restrict booths to building within a foot or two of the perimeter.

The discussions above offer the meeting planner a solid overview of trade-show development. Although space limitations prohibit a more detailed explanation of show rules and regulations, you will find that, even with more lengthy presentations, the rules vary so widely from one show to the next that the information, though voluminous, is too narrowly focused to be useful.

Exhibitor Violations and Dirty Tricks

Although security for your exhibitors is discussed in chapter 6, one situation that occurs on many exhibit hall floors is not so easily solved or detected, even by show management: psychological game playing.

Consider the thousands or even hundreds of thousands of dollars that an exhibiting company spends to attend your show. For a company to commit its resources to such an extent, clearly the opportunity for substantial enhancement of its profits must be readily apparent and the stakes high. Competition on the exhibit floor goes beyond ostentatious exhibits, elaborate booth decor, and well-dressed salespeople—the tangibles. Elusive subterfuge also goes on.

For example, an exhibitor might purchase attendee badges that are a different color from exhibitor badges and distribute them to several persons either on staff or hired expressly for the dirty trick. The tricksters then enter the exhibit

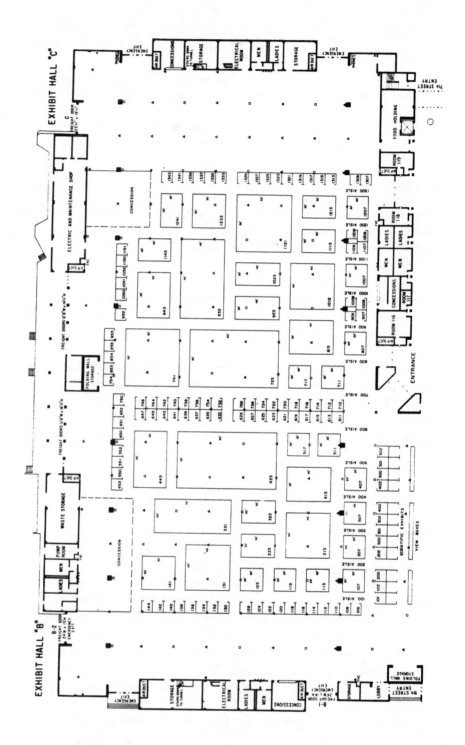

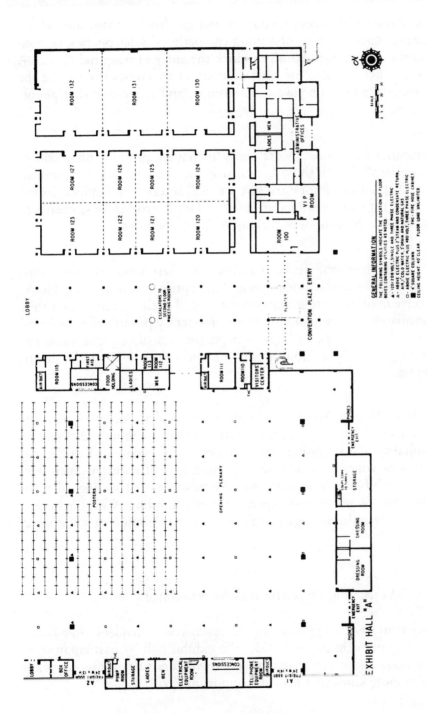

Figure 5-2. *Exhibit hall after booths have been assigned.* Reprinted with permission of the Freeman Decorating Companies, Houston, TX

floor under the guise of attendees or buyers and are free to roam the exhibit floor, investigating other exhibits, observing competitors' sales pitches, or congregating outside a competitor's booth to block the entry of potential clients. A show manager can keep control of such a situation by constantly roving the exhibit floor, keeping an eye on suspicious groups, and requesting that people keep the aisles free.

Banning Unauthorized Sessions. Most show managers prohibit off-premises "educational meetings" during show hours. It is the show manager's responsibility to ensure that all exhibitors are given equal access to attendees during exhibit hours. The off-site functions are usually lavish productions, meant to lure attendees off the exhibit floor and away from competitors.

Enlisting Help from Members. To keep a check on these kinds of operations, enlist the help of the association's members and the hotels in your housing block. If members receive invitations to unauthorized special events, request that they notify you immediately. In many organizations, monetary penalties are imposed for this type of violation. If the violation is repeated at a subsequent show, the show manager may close the exhibit in question and refuse to allow the exhibitor to show again.

Enlisting Help from Hotels. Write into hotel contracts that the hotel management will notify you of any requests for meeting rooms or food-and-beverage service in hospitality suites during show hours from persons identified as being participants of your show or from the same type of industry. Such persons could be nonexhibitors who want to take advantage of having all your attendees in town but do not want to spend money exhibiting. With the hotel's cooperation, unauthorized meetings can be kept to a minimum or eliminated entirely.

Marketing Opportunities for Exhibitors

Exhibitors enjoy being given opportunities to reach your attendees after hours and to display their name in places besides the exhibit hall by participating in sponsorship offerings and other programs. Following are suggestions for ways to give exhibitors these kinds of marketing opportunities.

Sponsorship Offerings

Many show managers offer their exhibitors various opportunities to promote their products—through sponsorship of parties, a tag line printed on registration badges, use of promotional shopping bags, and numerous other marketing ploys that enhance a convention with services or items that are not normally offered by the exhibiting organization because of the expense involved in purchasing these amenities.

Establishing Guidelines. Guidelines should be established regarding the availability and implementation of a sponsorship program. The following suggestions can be used as is or adapted to suit a particular show:

1. Each sponsorship will be offered for two years running, with the option not to purchase it the second year.

2. After two years, the particular sponsorship will again be offered to all exhibitors.

3. Any company that does not exhibit will be ineligible to purchase a sponsorship.

4. All sponsorships may include a tag line such as "With the compliments of . . ." and a booth number but no advertisement per se.

Devising a Format for Sponsorship Offerings. The sponsored items should be listed with costs of partial or entire sponsorship—for example, morning coffee breaks in the exhibit hall for all of the show days, $6,000; individual morning coffee breaks, $1,500. Other items that can be offered for sponsorship include registration portfolios, pens, writing pads, dance bands or entertainment at parties, speakers, and shuttle-bus routes.

User Meetings

Many associations offer opportunities for exhibitors to do a more thorough selling job to targeted attendees by allowing exhibitors to hold *user meetings,* that is, meetings that are miniseminars on exhibitors' products, offered to attendees during authorized hours in the convention center. This kind of opportunity is especially welcomed by those exhibitors which have merchandise needing more than just a brief sales pitch to educate buyers, and it eliminates off-site, illegal meetings.

Implementing User Meetings. The most practical way to handle user meetings is to make use of meeting rooms that are already set up the day before the show is officially opened. These rooms can then serve as seminar rooms for exhibitors.

Charging an Administration Fee. Many meeting planners charge an administration fee to offset any costs involved in planning user meetings. The fee covers postage, on-site management, and the printing of any signs used in conjunction with the user meetings.

Exhibitor Preview Meetings

Another effective way to offer service and to market your meeting to exhibitors is by organizing and holding an *exhibitor preview meeting*—a marketing technique that has proved to be a boon for all participants involved in a trade show or convention. Although most people involved in the meeting-planning industry possess the skills necessary to plan a convention, only a few seem to be using exhibitor preview meetings.

By creative marketing of an organization's meeting, a meeting planner attempts to attract the maximum number of attendees to the show and to individual exhibits. Although you cannot ensure automatic attendance at any booth, you can offer help by suggesting ways exhibitors can enhance their visibility to buyers, on and off the exhibit floor.

Exhibitors know, naturally, how to sell their product but do not necessarily understand or have the time to cope with all the details involved in planning special events for your attendees. Events like receptions and parties, together with the subsequent contracting with hotels for ballrooms, hospitality suites, or housing of company VIPs, may require outside assistance. Make these tasks easier for exhibitors by involving the hotels, local ground operators or destination management companies, special events companies, the convention center, the show director, and other suppliers by introducing your exhibitors to these contacts. The easiest way to get everyone involved is through personal introductions at the exhibitor preview meeting.

By helping your exhibitors to plan better parties and events, you will be assisting them to make your show more exciting for your attendees, which in turn will attract even more attendees—and more attendees mean better leads for exhibitors. Further, the bigger the parties, the more valuable your show becomes to hotels in terms of food-and-beverage and room sales. As the meeting planner, your financial clout is increased by using your exhibitors as leverage.

Your goal, besides helping your exhibitors, is to set up a field of "friendly competition"—competition among the participating hotels for your exhibitors' business and competition among your exhibitors for the best sites for events and housing.

Planning and Implementing the Meeting. An exhibitor preview meeting is typically held four to five weeks after the organization's current annual event, that is, about a year before your next event. An invitation is sent to all exhibitors, asking them to join you in the city that will be hosting next year's meeting. Included in the invitation is a housing form listing all the hotels in your housing block.

Notifying Hotels. Prior to mailing the invitations to exhibitors, telephone your sales contacts at all the hotels that will be participating in your housing block to apprize them of your plans to hold an exhibitor preview meeting. Then immediately follow your call with an official notification, *in memo format,* to the sales contacts, explaining their role in the exhibitor preview meeting and requesting their support.

Stress Marketing Opportunities. Your memo should emphasize the marketing and sales opportunities that will be available to the hotels: a captive audience of exhibitors eager not only to obtain the best accommodations for their VIPs and staff but to book the best ballrooms and hospitality suites in which to entertain members and delegates.

Request Complimentary Accommodations. After clearly stating the benefits of participating, your memo should (a) request complimentary accommodations for exhibitors that will be attending the meeting and (b) state that in return, the hotel representative will be given a five- to ten-minute time slot at the meeting in which to make a presentation to the group.

Ask Contacts to Bring Sales Tools. Suggest that the sales contacts bring brochures; menus; slides or videos of theme parties, special events, and food-and-beverage displays; information about any special features the hotel would like exhibitors to know about, such as ballrooms, hospitality suites, fine dining establishments, health spas, and a pool; and any historical items that would add interest to the presentation.

Why You Should Use the Memo Format. The memo format works best because it lists all participating hotels. This is a subtle but effective way to induce some friendly competition among the hotels and results in better understanding of the meeting, as well as cooperation among all hotels.

Involving General Managers. Involve general managers in your plans by sending another memo to the general managers of the participating hotels to remind them that their hotel will be housing your group and to briefly explain the exhibitor preview meeting and its goals. Attach a copy of the memo you wrote to the sales representatives, and extend an invitation to the general managers to join the group at the presentations.

Sample Memos for the Exhibitor Preview Meeting

Memo to the Hotels' General Managers:
To: (List all general managers)
From: Meeting planner
Re: Exhibitor preview meeting luncheon

Because you are participants in our housing block for our upcoming annual meeting, I want to give you an update on the meeting and tell you about our exhibitor preview meeting luncheon.

We are currently going into our 1989 show in (city), with all thirty-five hundred hotel rooms sold and with 10,000 more square feet of exhibit space sold than was sold in our previous meeting in (city), for a total of 60,000 square feet of exhibit space.

Over the past few years we have developed several new strategies that have enhanced our relationships not only with our exhibitors but with properties participating in our housing block as well. One plan in particular—the exhibitor preview meeting luncheon, which we have scheduled for (date)—will, I think, be of special interest to you. On that date, I will be visiting (city) with our most prestigious exhibitors. These exhibitors will be viewing the convention center and the headquarters hotel and inspecting other sites for special events. I have asked my sales and banquet contacts at each of your properties to meet with our exhibitors on (date) at the exhibitor preview meeting luncheon to distribute menus and hotel brochures and to give a five- to ten-minute presentation about their property, using either slides or a video display. In past

---

meetings, hotels have used slides of their suites, ballrooms, theme parties, and special banquet displays.

As you can see, this meeting gives our organization an opportunity to offer a service to our exhibitors—that is, to introduce them to our suppliers, thereby saving them time and energy in tracking down sites and contacts for their special events, receptions, banquets, and hospitality suites. And the properties appreciate the opportunity to meet our top exhibitors face to face and find the meeting a lucrative marketing vehicle. (As a follow-up to this meeting, I send each property a complete list of all exhibitors, including the ones that were not able to attend.)

For your information, I have enclosed the memo that was sent to all my contacts at your properties. These individuals will be attending the exhibitor preview meeting luncheon, and they have all responded enthusiastically to our invitation and to our request for complimentary accommodations for our exhibitors.

If your schedules permit, perhaps you could join us at the luncheon.

Memo to Hotel Sales Directors:

To: (List individually all sales contacts)
From: Meeting planner
Re: Exhibitor preview meeting luncheon

Thank you all for your enthusiastic response to my phone call this week about our exhibitor preview meeting luncheon to be held (time, place, date).

I will be forwarding the final housing list to you shortly. As of today, the exhibitors who are attending are as follows: (list exhibitors).

(Destination management company contact) will be handling the logistics of the luncheon and arranging for transportation of exhibitors from the convention center to the (luncheon site). Please call (name) at (number) to coordinate your slide- or video-presentation time during the luncheon.

Thank you again for your participation. I am looking forward to meeting you all in (city).

Inviting the Destination Management Company and Convention and Visitor's Bureau. Also send a similar invitation to the destination management company with which you will be working. Include with your invitation a request for a complimentary shuttle bus for use during the meeting. The convention and visitors bureau representative should be asked to open the luncheon with a welcome from the city.

Scheduling the Meeting. Following is a rundown of recommended times and events for the meeting.

- *8:30–10:00*A.M. The meeting begins with breakfast in a meeting room of the designated headquarters hotel. Present are all exhibitors, the show decorator, and the meeting planner. The new, tentative floor plans are displayed. All exhibitors are invited to step up and discuss the new plans and review any possible changes in booth size, problems with the site, and so on.

- *10:00–10:30*A.M. All depart the hotel for the convention center, boarding the complimentary bus for the trip. On the bus, the representatives from the destination management company are given an opportunity to point out the special features of the bus and to mention that this is the type of bus that will be used by the hosting association for shuttle service during the convention. If time permits, a brief tour of the city is conducted and special sites for nonhotel events—riverboats, museums, galleries, and so on—are highlighted. The speaker gives pertinent information on these sites (number of people that can be accommodated at a sit-down dinner, reception, party, and so forth) and explains that by working directly with the company for these events—or even for planning part of the event or just supplying props for theme parties—the exhibitors will avoid duplicating themes or setting conflicting dates.

- *10:30*A.M.*–12:00 noon.* The group arrives at the convention center. A walk-through of the exhibit halls and meeting rooms is conducted. Fire and safety restrictions and traffic flow are discussed, and banquet and food-and-beverage information is distributed.

- *12:00 noon–12:30*P.M. Everyone boards the bus for the trip to the reception/luncheon site. (Quite often, the destination management company, in conjunction with an elegant restaurant or club suitable for exhibitor events, will offer to host a luncheon for the exhibitors. These sites are rarely seen by exhibitors, since they haven't the time to scout around, or such sites are open only to members. In the case of private clubs, destination management companies are often the only ones with access to these sites, a point that should be stressed during the trip to the luncheon, in addition to presenting the highlights of the hosting property.) Upon arrival, the group is escorted to the reception area, where all the hotel contacts will be waiting. The time spent in the reception area is used by the meeting planner to attempt to pair each exhibitor with the most suitable property.

- *12:30–2:00P.M.* Lunch is announced, and everyone moves to the luncheon area, which is set up with a projector and screen, as well as a podium and microphone if necessary. Everyone is served the first course without interruption. Between the first course and the entrée, the representative of the convention and visitors bureau makes the welcoming remarks, thanking the group for coming. (These remarks could be followed by a video, if available, about the city.) The meeting planner then begins introducing the hotel representatives. By the time coffee and dessert are finished, all presentations will have been made. Packets with menus and brochures are distributed. The meeting planner and destination management company distribute a list of nonhotel sites, with capacities and locations from the hotels in the housing block and any other information that would be helpful for exhibitors that want to plan a party. Business cards are exchanged, good-byes are spoken, and the bus is waiting to drop everyone off at either the hotels or the airport.

Post–Exhibitor Preview Meeting Procedures. You should send individual thank-you notes to all participants; included with your note should be a list of all exhibitors that did not attend the meeting. Next, send an announcement to all nonparticipating exhibitors, telling them how sorry you are that they were unable to attend (and mentioning how successful the meeting was for the attendees, who obtained the best party sites, hospitality suites, and so on) but stating that you have sent their names to all the contacts in the city.

By incorporating an exhibitor preview meeting into your overall service package for exhibitors, I am sure you will experience all the benefits of this unique and exciting marketing tool.

Managing a trade show is a multifaceted endeavor. It begins with a floor plan and ends with service—service to your exhibitors, attendees, and suppliers. All three principals will respond and participate actively and enthusiastically to the level of spirit, professionalism, and creativity shown by the convention manager.

6
Safety and Security: Developing a Security Plan, Evaluating Security Companies, Developing a Security-Needs Flow Chart, Educating Exhibitors about Security, Planning for Attendee Security

S afety and security are important considerations when planning a meeting of any size, but they take on monumental proportions when planning a convention. The personal safety and security of attendees while they are at the convention center and as they travel around the city are the responsibility of the convention manager, as is exhibitor security—that is, the measures that must be taken to protect exhibitor merchandise.

Security is an expensive item; for a large show, costs can run into thousands of dollars. This chapter will show you how to plan for security in the most economical manner while not skimping on this substantial aspect of convention management.

Security in the Exhibit Hall

Planning for your security needs in the convention center begins with a site inspection scheduled twelve to eighteen months before your show's arrival.

Most large convention centers have a full-time, in-house staff to manage security in the building and on the premises, including parking lots, lobbies, loading docks, and the grounds surrounding the complex.

Hiring a Security Company

In addition to the house security, you will need your own security force. This service can be hired through the security company already on-site, if the company offers that service, or you can hire your own force to work with the house security company. Whichever method you choose, you must analyze your needs and prepare a specification sheet to be submitted with a request for a proposal.

Requesting a Proposal

When requesting a proposal from a security firm, include the following information about the show:

- Description of your show's attendees—for example, lawyers, engineers, or writers

- Expected number of attendees

- Number and size of exhibits, plus a description of the exhibits themselves—jewelry, computers, books, and so forth.

- Any information that is unusual, specific, or unique to the show (for instance, one-of-a-kind prototypes, rare books)

- The particular security concerns of exhibitors (for example, exhibitors of antique jewelry would naturally be concerned with theft, but exhibitors involved with scientific technology or medical instrumentation would be more concerned with industrial sabotage)

In the case of a jewelry show, you would need visible, uniformed guards specifically trained for and knowledgeable about sleight-of-hand thievery. By contrast, a show featuring new scientific material would require security measures geared to after-hours break-ins by people with a knowledge of high technology and armed with cameras. You can't assume that a security agency is sophisticated enough to realize that the results of such a theft of technology and scientific ideas could represent many years of research and enormous sum of money.

Examining Security Needs during Move-in/Move-out

The most demanding time for security personnel is move-in and move-out. The activities immediately preceding and following a convention are a security nightmare. Multitudes of people are swarming the exhibit hall floor and meeting rooms. Carpenters, electricians, forklift drivers, executives from the exhibiting companies, audiovisual technicians—are all coming and going throughout the day and night. Include in your specification sheet a timetable of your move-in/move-out phases, and ask for precise recommendations for these periods.

Preparing a Cover Letter

When the specification sheet is complete, prepare a cover letter to the prospective security agency outlining the date and location of your meeting. Specify whether you will be using the entire convention center or just a portion of the building, as well as what public areas will be occupied—for example, registration areas, restaurants, and meeting rooms. Then add a proposed budget parameter and a request for several suggestions on various security plans. Your final statement should request a list of references and give a cutoff date for receipt of the proposal.

Evaluating the Proposal

Be prepared to spend time analyzing a security company's proposal. Look for suggestions from the company's representative, not just a replay of your specifications with a price tag. If you are concerned with technology theft or industrial sabotage, the proposal should contain specific recommendations relating to the layout of the hall. And because the hours before and after a show can cause as least as many security problems as the actual show hours can, the security company's proposal should include costs and suggestions for the evening hours as well.

Evaluating Staff Training and Experience

A critical factor in deciding on a security firm is the depth of staff experience and the method of staff training. Most security companies draw their employees from a general pool of candidates. This type of employee is fine for checking badges, taking tickets, and dealing with lost or confused attendees. But just because the employee is dressed in a uniform does not necessarily mean that he or she is experienced in blending tactful treatment and enforcement or is conversant with the ways of thieves. Low bids could mean low wages for the guards. And because people with experience demand higher salaries, a good indication of the quality of staff training and experience may be the total bid.

Evaluating the Supervisor

If your show does not place intense demands on the security force, you may want to concern yourself only with the degree of training of the on-site supervisor. However, the supervisor should be knowledgeable about the facility in order to answer questions and should be expected to behave diplomatically when confronted with the inevitable disgruntled registrant. Ideally, the supervisor should be drawn from the ranks of off-duty or retired police officers trained in crowd-control methods, the handling of unwanted intruders, and other sensitive situations.

Assessing the Honesty of Security Staff

Security staff, like the various people coming and going on the exhibit floor, may or may not be averse to taking merchandise. The safeguards against this type of theft are certainly worth discussing before you hire a security firm. Although there are no guarantees of any individual's honesty, a security firm should bond its employees, screen them for criminal records and substance abuse, and conduct a thorough background check.

Contacting References

Before making a final decision on a company, call all the references it has supplied. Speak with individual meeting planners, asking for their opinions of and experiences with the security firm. Keep notes on all discussions. Just because one meeting planner had a bad experience doesn't mean the security firm was at fault. If the proper information was not submitted or the meeting planner did not clearly communicate the requirements to the security coordinator, an unsatisfactory situation could have resulted. A lack of sufficient understanding about costs or unrealistic expectations on the part of the meeting planner regarding service for price could be at the root of the problem (which is why a comprehensive specification sheet is so important). If you receive negative feedback from more than one or two meeting planners, you can call the convention center or the convention and visitors bureau for further verification of facts.

Finalizing the Agreement

When you feel that one proposal satisfies all your needs and the references are in order, request a contract from the particular security company. When the contract arrives, closely compare it with the original proposal to determine that all points have been covered as originally stated.

On-site Management

Move-in/Move-out. All personnel entering and leaving the convention center during move-in and move-out should be issued color-coded badges and instructed to wear them at all times. All security guards should be given a badge-coding list and told to question any inconsistencies with approved procedure. A badge-coding list might look something like this:

Red: Exhibitors

Green: Crew

Blue: Show decorator crew

Brown: Hired labor (carpenters, plumbers, and so on)

Purple: Guests

Property Removal Passes. Any personnel exiting the convention center with packages or bags should be asked to sign a property removal sheet and should be issued a property removal pass. The sheet should contain the person's name, affiliation, and driver's license identification number; the time and date the pass is issued; a legible signature of the property holder; and the guard's name.

Skulduggery. Watch your trash? Yes, it sounds strange, but there could be money in those trash dumpsters. The most useful items show up in trash bins; computers, audiovisual equipment, exhibitor merchandise. It's an old scam, but forewarned is forearmed. Security should be instructed to check all "empty boxes" and "trash" going into dumpsters.

Secured Areas. Many exhibit halls offer exhibitors *security cages.* These cages resemble the kinds of cages used for large animals. Some cages are movable and can be used on the exhibit floor during move-in and move-out. Exhibitors keep these cages next to their exhibits to store valuables when they are away from the exhibit hall during move-in/move-out or overnight.

Individual Exhibitor Security. Not all exhibitors think about security. New and inexperienced exhibitors should be educated about security issues and given an opportunity to review their needs with the show manager. To assume a level of knowledge that your exhibitors may not possess isn't in their best interests and can ultimately cause you problems that could have been avoided with proper education before their arrival at the exhibit hall.

The following informational memo can be used as is or adapted to suit the needs of your show's exhibitors. Educating your exhibitors, especially in the area of security, will have long-reaching and beneficial effects for the continued growth of your show.

Memo[a]

To: All exhibitors
From: Show manager
Re: Security

This memo is written in an effort to keep our exhibitors well informed about security practices in general and about those at our upcoming event (name, date, city) in particular.
Guard Services
Show management will have a perimeter guard service in the facility twenty-four hours a day, including all setup, exposition, and dismantling hours. *You are reminded, however, that the primary responsibility for safeguarding your exhibit and your merchandise is yours.* While show management will exercise reasonable care in safeguarding your property, neither

[a]The memo was created by Maribeth Kraus, Director of Technical Exhibits and Continuing Education, Society of Nuclear Medicine. (Printed with permission.)

show management nor the facility, security contractor, drayage contractor, or any of their officers, agents, or employees assume any responsibility for such property.

Professional security-guard service will be provided on an around-the-clock basis beginning with the first day of move-in (date) and continuing until the exhibit hall is vacated (date). Each party involved in the exhibit—exhibit hall owner, leasing organization (association name), and exhibitor—agrees to be responsible for any claims arising out of its own negligence or that of its employees or agents.

Badging System

The badging system is an essential ingredient of the security program at our event. Therefore, show management has instructed security personnel to allow, at the appropriate times, only badged personnel within the exhibition area. The basic rule is that under no circumstances will anyone be allowed on the exhibit floor without proper identification. We ask your cooperation and attention in complying with this system, for it is to the benefit of all concerned.

Official badges for exhibitors will be limited to (number, per the association's choosing) for each 100 square feet contracted. Admission to the exhibit hall for booth exhibitors and attendees will be by badge only; the exhibit hall will be closed to the public. Please preregister your representatives when you receive the exhibitor service kit. Only individuals who work in an exhibitor's booth can have an exhibitor's badge.

Attendance after Show Hours during Show Dates

To ensure maximum security protection, no after-hours work or entertainment will be permitted in the exhibit booths unless approved by show management.

Cameras

All cameras will be banned in the exhibit hall during nonshow hours. Photographs can be taken only by the official show photographer or by a photographer contracted by the individual exhibitor. In the latter case, the exhibitor must treat the photographer as it would any other outside contractor: supplying name, address, and supervisor in attendance, along with the names of personnel employed and the appropriate insurance certificates. A list of these photographers will be given to security, and the photographers will be allowed only in the booth for which they were contracted.[b]

Evening Admission to Exhibit Hall

A list of persons desiring evening admission to the exhibit hall must be submitted prior to 5:00 P.M. for approval by show management or its duly appointed representatives. Show management reserves the right to limit the

---

[b]This paragraph is more often included for high-technology shows.

time such personnel will be allowed to work. The guard on duty will receive copies of these lists and be authorized to control the individuals' access to the hall. In addition, all such personnel must sign in and out on the evening admission sheet whenever they leave or enter the hall.

Insurance

Exhibitors should be aware that neither show management nor the facility, security contractor, drayage contractor, or any of their officers, agents, or employees assume any responsibility for exhibitors' property. Exhibitors should include in their insurance policies (or have a rider attached to them) coverage for the shipment of merchandise to the convention center, for the period of the convention, and for the return of their merchandise to their home base.

Each party agrees to be responsible for its own property through insurance or self-insurance and shall hold harmless each of the other parties for any and all damage caused by theft and those perils normally covered by a fire-and-extended-coverage policy.

Security Precautions

Please bear in mind that your exhibit merchandise and displays are your prime selling tools. It is therefore of utmost importance that you take every precaution to protect this material. Toward this end, here are a few suggestions:

1. Ship in locked trunks or crates.

2. If you use cartons, be sure they are security taped or banded; under no circumstances should you mark on the outside the name or type of articles contained in the cartons.

3. Ship with a qualified trucker or forwarder. Do not hire your shipper solely on price. A company that may, in its proposal appear inexpensive, could, after further investigation, be found to have inadequate or no insurance; to use unbonded, unreliable, or unskilled workers; or to have disreputable drivers, unsafe equipment, or equipment inadequate for your needs.

4. Be sure to furnish your shipping company with an accurate and complete bill of lading.

5. Do not leave your booth unattended during the setup period.

6. Cover your display after setup and each night before you leave. If your merchandise is particularly valuable, consider private security.

7. Do not under any circumstances include merchandise in containers to be stored with empties.

8. At the close of the exposition, be sure to pack as quickly as possible. Under no circumstances should you leave your space unattended during this period.

9. Have one of your employees remain in your space with your shipment until it is actually picked up by the drayage contractor's (shipping) personnel.

Property Removal Pass. Any individual removing property from the exhibit hall at any time will be required to have a property removal pass designating what merchandise is to be removed and by whose authorization. This pass, which can be obtained from show management, the show decorator, or security, must be submitted to the guard.

On-site Needs Assessment

Once you have contracted with a security company, you must begin defining your specific needs for on-site security.

To determine exactly what those needs are, conduct a walk-through of the entire convention center with the in-house or other security company's representative, your show decorator, your audiovisual supervisor, and the facility's convention services manager. Walk through the entire building—exhibit hall, meeting rooms, lounge areas, restaurants, rest rooms, registration areas, elevators, escalators, loading docks, entry ramps outside parking lots, and so on. Note public entrances and nonpublic or service entrances. Carry a floor plan of each area, and note on the floor plans (by number) where you will need your security and what type of security you will need. In the case of shows for which there is a need for top-level security precautions, such as government or military expositions or shows exhibiting high-technology equipment, this is the time to decide on the placement of X-ray scanning devices, electronic frisking equipment, and cameras and to work out issues of traffic flow or bottlenecks.

Developing a Security-Needs Flow Chart

After completing the walk-through, devise a flow chart that incorporates all the notations you made on the floor plans.

The following example of a security-needs flow chart can be adapted to any show's requirements, adding or reducing elements to suit individual needs.

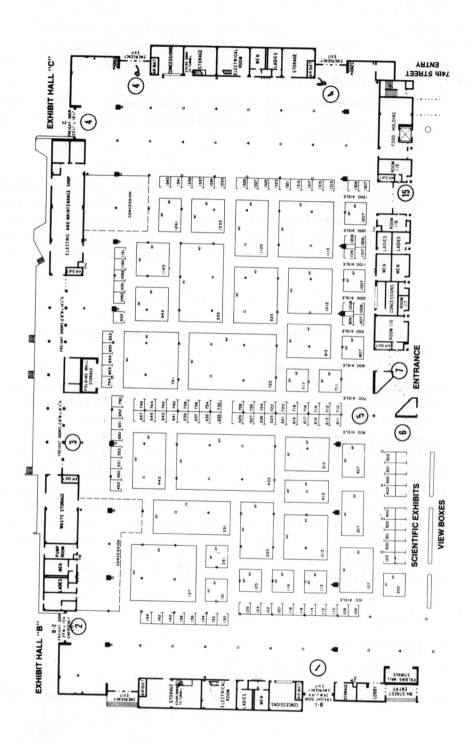

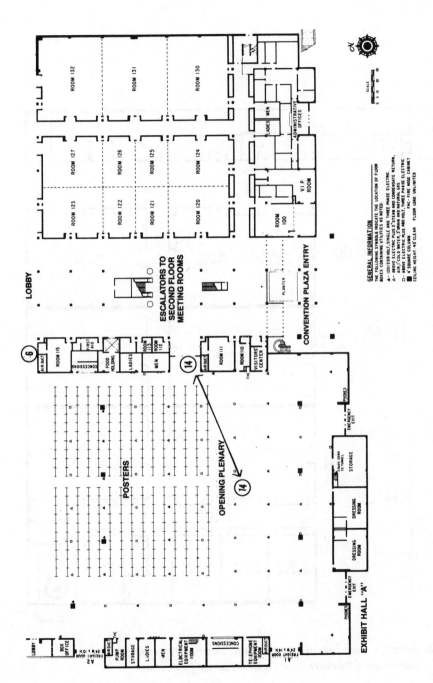

Figure 6–1. *Floor plan for security guard stations numbered to correspond with security flow chart*

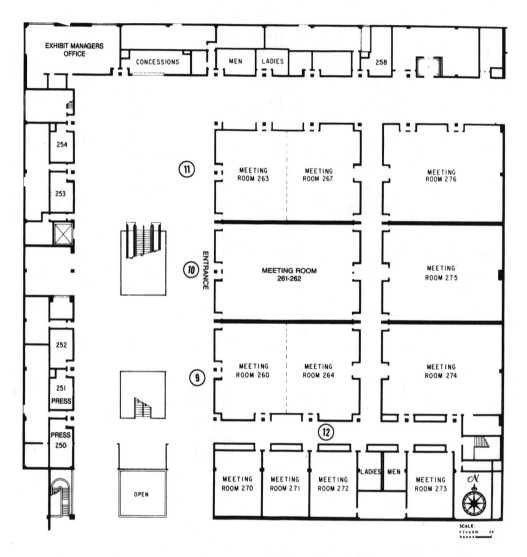

Figure 6–2. *Security guard stations on second floor of the convention center numbered to correspond with security flow chart*

Sta.	Description	Thurs 6/8	Fri 6/9	Sat 6/10	Sun 6/11	Mon 6/12	Tues 6/13	Wed 6/14	Thurs 6/15	Fri 6/16	Sat 6/17	Sun 6/18
1	B-1 Drive-In Frght. Ent. Hall B	12N–6P	7:30A–6P	7:30A–5P	7:30A–5P					12N–11P	7:30A–12M	7:30A–12N
2	Frght Ent. Hall B	12N–6P	7:30A–6P	7:30A–5P	7:30A–5P	6:30A–5P				12N–11P	7:30A–12M	7:30A–12N
3	B-C Dock	12N–6P	7:30A–6P	7:30A–5P	7:30A–5P	6:30A–5P	6:30A–5:30P	6:30A–5:30P	6:30A–5:30P	12N–11P	7:30A–12M	6:30A–12N
4	Drive-In Freight Entrance/Hall C	12N–6P	7:30A–6P	7:30A–5P	7:30A–5P					12N–11P	7:30A–12M	7:30A–12N
4 a&b	Emergency Exits Hall C						6:30A–5:30P (Badge Ckr.)	6:30A–5:30P	6:30A–5:30P	6:30A–1P		
5	Exhibit Halls A, B, C Roving Officer (Armed Off-Duty Officer only on evening shift)	12N–on (Halls B&C)	24 hours (Halls B&C)	24 hours	24 hours (Halls A, B, C)	24 hours	24 hours	24 hours	24 hours	24 hours	7:30A–12M	7:30A ----12N
6	Exhibit Hall Entrance to A						6:30A–7:30P (Badge Ckr.)	6:30A–7:30P	6:30A–7:30P	6:30A–12:30P		
6a	Bet. Commercial & Scientific Exhibits						6:30A–10A	6:30A–10A	6:30A–10A	6:30A–8:30A		

Figure 6–3. Security flow chart

Sta.	Description	Thurs 6/8	Fri 6/9	Sat 6/10	Sun 6/11	Mon 6/12	Tues 6/13	Wed 6/14	Thurs 6/15	Fri 6/16	Sat 6/17	Sun 6/18
7	Exhibit Hall Main Entrance to B & C	12N–6P	7:00A– 10P (Badge Checker)	7:00A– 10P (Badge Checker)	7:00A– 10P (Badge Checker)	6:30A– 10P (Badge Checker)	6:30A– 5:30P (2 Badge Checkers)	6:30A– 5:30P (2 Badge Checkers)	6:30A– 5:30P (2 Badge Checkers)	6:30A– 11P (Badge Checker)		
8	Registration Area			12N on	24 hours	24 hours	24 hours	24 hours	24 hours	To 6P		
9	Room 260– 2nd Floor					7A–12N (2 ticket-takers)						
10	Room 261– 2nd Floor					7A–12N (2 ticket-takers)						
11	Room 263– 2nd Floor					7A–12P (2 ticket-takers)						
12	Room 272– 2nd Floor					7A–12P (2 ticket-takers)						
13	EMS Technition					8A–5P	8A–5P	8A–5P	8A–5P	8A–5P		
14	Exhibit Hall A					5P–8A (Inside Hall) 8A– 10:30A at door						
15	Exhibit Hall C Bet. Rms 118 & 119						10A– 5:30P	10A– 5:30P	10A– 5:30P	8:30A– 11P		

Figure 6–3. *continued*

	Station	Thur 6/8	Fri 6/9	Sat 6/10	Sun 6/11	Mon 6/12	Tues 6/13	Wed 6/14	Thur 6/15	Fri 6/16	Sat 6/17	Sun 6/18
Building Open	1	12N	7:30A	7:30A	7:30A	Locked	Locked	Locked	Locked	12N	7:30A	7:30A
	2	12N	7:30A	7:30A	7:30A	6:30A	Locked	Locked	Locked	12N	7:30A	7:30A
	3	12N	7:30A	7:30A	7:30A	6:30A	Locked	Locked	Locked	12N	7:30A	7:30A
	4	12N	7:30A	7:30A	7:30A	Locked	Locked	Locked	Locked	12N	7:30A	7:30A
	4 a&b	Locked	------	------	------	------	6:30A	6:30A	6:30A	6:30A	Locked	Locked
	6	Locked	------	------	------	------	6:30A	6:30A	6:30A	6:30A	Locked	------
	7	12N	7A	7A	7A	6:30A	6:30A	6:30A	6:30A	6:30A	6:30A	6:30A
	15	Locked	------	------	------	Locked	10A	10A	10A	10A	8:30A	Locked
	Convention Pl.	12N	6A	6A	6A	6A	6A	6A	6A	6A	6A	6A
Building Lock-Up	1	6P	6P	5P	5P	Locked	Locked	Locked	Locked	11P	12M	12N
	2	6P	6P	5P	5P	5P	5:30P	5:30P	5:30P	11P	12M	12N
	3	6P	6P	5P	5P	5P	5:30P	5:30P	5:30P	11P	12M	12N
	4	6P	6P	5P	5P	Locked	Locked	Locked	Locked	11P	12M	12N
	4 a&b	Locked	------	------	------	------	5:30P	5:30P	5:30P	1P	Locked	------
	6	6P	10P	10P	10P	10P	7:30P	7:30P	7:30P	12:30P	Locked	------
	7	Locked	10P	10P	10P	10P	5:30P	5:30P	5:30P	11P	Locked	------
	15	Locked	------	------	------	------	5:30P	5:30P	5:30P	11P	Locked	------
	Convention Pl.	As requested										

Figure 6–4. *Facility access and lock-up time chart*

Such a chart is an excellent reference for your specification sheet when you are submitting information to security firms for future requests for proposals. Pay special attention to that part of the flow chart which outlines day-to-day information regarding lock up of doors and exits.

Following Up

After the security-needs flow chart and floor plan is complete, send copies to your security coordinator, the facility's convention services manager, the in-house security company, your show decorator, and your audiovisual supervisor for troubleshooting and verification that you have incorporated all the points covered during the walk-through. Handling security in this manner not only will give you an accurate picture of your final costs but will also make adjustments, additions, or deletions simple and accurate and will allow you to communicate efficiently and concisely with all on-site personnel.

Protocol

The walk-through is an excellent time to discuss protocol with both the in-house security supervisor and your contracted security representative. Make notes on house procedures for fire alarms, evacuation, and medical emergencies. Familiarize yourself with the procedures. When assigning staff members to handle on-site communications, convey this information to them orally and in writing.

Individual Safety

An unpleasant incident experienced by an attendee, exhibitor, or staff member will quickly ruin the atmosphere of even the most smoothly running show. A comprehensive security and safety plan would be incomplete without consideration of individual safety issues—that is, information for your attendees, staff, and exhibitors that is unique to the particular city and convention center, as well as basic, away-from-home, commonsense advice. It is unwise for a meeting planner to assume on the part of attendees a level of travel sophistication that may not exist; it is always better to give them too much rather than too little information.

An easy and effective method of alerting people to site-specific problems is to post a map of the city in the convention center lobby, marking the unsafe areas as redlines. Highlight suggested walking routes to and from the various hotels to the convention center, as well as any routes people may use to travel to nightlife areas and shopping districts. This map can also be inserted into the registration portfolios or handed out when people are given their badges.

Use of Restaurant Guides to Steer Attendees to Safe Neighborhoods. Many show managers develop a restaurant guide for each city. With personal computers and word processors, this is a relatively easy production. Information can be obtained from the convention and visitors bureau; local members of your association are a good source of information too. Attendees will make use of these guides, especially if data on prices and dress codes are included. It is important that you check any information you receive from local members and friends with the convention and visitors bureau to verify that the restaurants are not in high-crime areas. Sending a tourist into that kind of situation will offset all the good you are doing by offering the guide in the first place. The primary purpose of the guide is to steer out-of-towners to the safe parts of town; the secondary purpose is to offer information about eating establishments. Such a guide is a useful, inexpensive, and unobtrusive way to keep attendees safe.

Use of Shuttle Buses for Safety. Although shuttle buses are an expense, they pay off in peace of mind. In cities without safe, convenient public transportation or safe streets, shuttle busing is the most secure way to get attendees to and from the convention center. Using shuttle busing for your attendees' transportation needs will eliminate a great many chance happenings.

Note: Many organizations use a hotel rebate system that greatly offsets the cost of shuttle service. The procedure is simple and accepted by most hotels. During your discussions with a hotel sales representative, mention that you will be adding a rebate amount to your negotiated hotel rate, the published rate being $4 or $5 higher than the negotiated rate. Secure the hotel's permission and acceptance in writing. For example, let's say that you have negotiated a $95 rate at the XYZ Hotel. On your housing form, the rate will appear as $99. If the average stay of each attendee is four nights, that means $16 will be rebated to your association for each guest. If you have a thousand guests in that hotel all staying four nights, you will receive $16,000 from the hotel at the end of your show. If you are using eight, ten, or more hotels, you can see how the rebate— an essentially painless system for attendees, since not many people object to paying $4 or $5 a day for transportation—can generate enough funds to greatly reduce the cost of the shuttle-bus service. It is, however, very important that your housing form clearly notify attendees about such a rebate.

Commonsense Advice. Many meeting planners develop a list of commonsense rules for personal safety that they distribute to attendees by either inserting the flier into the registration portfolio or asking the hotel registration personnel to give the flier to attendees when they register. Following are recommended points to include in such a list:

1. Always use the peephole before opening the door to your hotel room.

2. If your room has a balcony, *when you first check in* ascertain that the lock works, and thereafter be sure to keep this door locked.

3. Always have a bellhop escort you to your room when you check in, even if you are carrying only one bag. Hotels are notorious for assigning one room to two separate parties. Walking into an already-occupied room can, at the least, be embarrassing.

4. Don't announce your room number across a crowded lobby or in the elevator. Crank callers need only a room number to do their job. Announcing your number and then getting off an elevator alone can invite unwanted problems as well.

5. Use valet parking—it's safer and worth the cost.

6. If you have to leave your bags unattended at the airport curbside or while you check in, secure them with a chain or cable and lock. Loop them together and secure them to something heavy or large.

7. Always ask a bellhop to tell you the safest route to your destination, if you are walking, and the approximate length of time it takes to get there by cab. If the bellhop suggests you take a cab, even for a short distance, take one.

8. Before you leave home, make copies of all your identification—passport, driver's license, credit cards, insurance cards—so that if they are lost or stolen, replacing them will be easier.

Public Disturbances

Although not likely to occur, demonstrations are a possibility at any show. It is wise to take a few minutes to map out a procedure to deal with demonstrators should an incident occur. The following guidelines are easily incorporated into a meeting management plan and easily implemented if the need arises.

1. Designate a spokesperson for the group.

2. If you feel there is a possibility of a disruption, meet with personnel from your headquarters hotel and the convention center.

3. If you feel that such an event is likely to occur, alert the local police of a possible demonstration.

4. If a protest does occur, have your designated spokesperson (who might turn out to be you) ask to speak with the group's spokesperson.

5. Try to avoid calling the police if an event does occur. You must, however, follow the advice of the security professionals at the hotel or convention center who may feel the situation requires police presence.

6. A democratic way of dealing with a dissenting group is to acknowledge that its members have a legitimate concern and to give them floor space and a table in your headquarters hotel and/or the convention center to display pamphlets and brochures. If your attendees are interested in the issue, they will then be free to approach the group and to read the material or discuss the issue.

Evacuation Procedures

A close scrutiny of the premises with the fire marshal and a knowledge of your show's attendees will give you ample information on procedures followed by individual convention centers, in the unlikely event of an emergency. If your show poses particular problems—for example, if it contains a large number of disabled persons, children, or animals—those considerations should be discussed with the fire marshal.

Medical Emergency Procedures

It is the show manager's responsibility to make sure that any on-site emergencies are dealt with in the most medically prudent manner. With the facilities management, discuss in detail what procedures are followed for various types of medical emergencies and ascertain how many on-site facility staff members are trained in first-aid and CPR procedures. Determine what hospitals serve the facility or are used for various emergencies, such as burns or heart attacks.

Developing a safety and security plan for your convention, exhibitors, and attendees will consume a great deal of time and effort. The information in this chapter should help you to focus on the major areas of concern and to understand those principals of security and safety which can be adapted to fit a show or meeting of any size.

7

On-site Communications: Developing a Complete Communications Network

This chapter concentrates on developing a telecommunications network for on-site management of a trade show.

Implementing a comprehensive communications plan is a necessity. It is important that all personnel directly involved with the on-site management of the show be in constant communication. The convention center is vast, the potential for safety, security, or management problems a constant presence. And in addition to management personnel, plans must also be made to facilitate communication among attendees on-site and among attendees, their families, and their workplace.

Components of a Communications Plan

The various channels of communication for a trade show are as follows:

- Management to attendee

- Management to management: convention manager to show decorator, convention center manager, audiovisual supervisor, security supervisor, and the organization's staff (also communications among all these persons)

- Attendee to attendee

- Attendee to show management

- Attendee to family, workplace, and outside world

In-house Communications

Public Address System

Implementing an efficient public address (PA) system is the priority of a comprehensive communications plan. The safety and well-being of all attendees and personnel on-site at a convention center are directly related to the staffing and management of a PA system.

The PA system should be run by one person. He or she should be trained and able to handle attendees' requests for PA access and to decide whether use is justified or not. Good show management restricts the use of the PA system to medical and safety emergencies.

Show Communications Center

In addition to a PA system, you will need a mechanism for instant and accurate communications among you, your convention services manager, your audiovisual supervisor, the show decorator, the security supervisor, and your staff. Establishing a central point of communication with someone designated as the expediter should be planned before the meeting takes place.

An excellent arrangement for a PA and communications management center is to designate a room that is easily accessible to convention center personnel, organization staff, and attendees. Such a room—usually called *office central* or *show central*—is equipped with two or three phones, each with two or three lines and all with the same number. The designated PA monitor staffs the phones in office central and is in constant two-way radio contact with the show manager, convention services manager, audiovisual supervisor, show decorator, and security supervisor. An additional staff member should be assigned to this post, both to be designated as runner and to relieve the PA monitor during breaks.

The phone number assigned to this room should not be made public; the room is not intended for use as a general message center. If the person staffing the message center (an entity discussed later in this chapter) is informed of a situation that may need a PA announcement, he or she can be instructed to give the office central number to the caller.

Office/show central is also used by show management to keep tabs on attendee problems and requests. Therefore, besides the PA monitor and his or her relief, additional personnel should be available to assist the monitor in contacting non-radio-equipped personnel or in the event of radio malfunction.

Finally, other staff members operating out of other service areas but not on radio—for example, personnel in the accounting department, pressroom, or registration area—should also use office central to keep in touch with the center of operations and to request assistance when needed.

Radios

It is up to the show manager to determine just how many staff members should be on radio. Radios are an indispensable communications tool for the primary managers of the show. And while you don't want to flood the airways with transmissions and thereby defeat the purpose of communications, a judicious allocation of radios is mandatory. Personnel you would want on one wavelength are the following:

- Show decorator. This person will also be equipped with a second radio to communicate with his or her own staff and crew.

- Convention services manager—your link to the entire service crew of the convention center as well as to house security and medical emergency staff. This person will work closely with you and your show decorator and audiovisual supervisor and will be constantly available to handle any building engineering or labor requirements.

- PA monitor.

- Exhibits manager.

- Show manager.

- Security supervisor. This person will have a radio tuned to the house security as well as your frequency.

A Typical Radio Event

The following "event" is an exaggerated scenario to demonstrate how a communications situation should be properly handled with radios.

Show exhibit manager from the exhibit floor to the audiovisual supervisor somewhere in the building: I have an exhibitor here who forgot that he needs twelve monitors by tomorrow morning. Over.

Office central monitor: Excuse me, exhibit manager, but I picked up your request. There was a large noise on this floor caused by equipment falling off a shelf. The audiovisual supervisor was here but probably didn't hear your transmission. I'll dispatch someone to tell him of your request. Over.

Audiovisual supervisor: This is the audiovisual supervisor. I heard the last transmission, the messenger is here, and I'm on my way to the exhibit floor. Over.

Show decorator: Exhibit manager, I heard your transmission. Your exhibitor will need more outlets in his booth. I'm sending an electrician over to meet with everyone. Over.

Convention services manager: Your exhibitor will need additional approval from the fire marshal. I've contacted her, and she's on her way to the booth. Over.

Radios save time and footsteps, and they avoid frustration. Just think how long the above communications would have taken were it not for radios. Even using the phones (called land lines in radio lingo) would not have facilitated things so quickly, since no one was near his or her office at the time of the transmissions.

Note: Please remember that when you communicate with radios, you are using public airways, and everyone with a radio—cabdrivers and police included—can hear what you say. The Federal Communications Commission has rulings that limit the expressions and exclamations that may first come to mind when one is faced with a crisis.

Handling False Alarms

It seems as though the imp of the preverse has full reign at conventions. No matter how sophisticated the system, fire and evacuation alarms have a way of being activated without provocation. Accordingly, a system should be established between your PA monitor and the convention services manager regarding the proper procedures to follow in such instances. Authorization that the occurrence is only a false alarm should come from one person on the convention center staff to only one responsible person operating the PA system.

The Message Center

A well-equipped, efficiently staffed message center provides a valuable and necessary service for your attendees. Either such a center can be staffed by your own personnel, or staff can be hired through the convention and visitors bureau.

Equipping a Message Center. The usual message center consists of a standard 20-by-20-foot pipe-and-drape booth in the main lobby or registration area. Poster boards are placed along the back of the booth, with A–Z cards posted along the top of the boards and ample space left for pinning messages beneath each letter. The booth is equipped with two, three, or more phones, all with the same number and keyed to incoming calls only. (Phones are so keyed to eliminate attendee requests to use the message center phone for returning calls.) The message center should be near a phone bank so that members can quickly return calls. The booth should also be stocked with paper, message pads, pencils, large waste baskets, and pushpins to post messages.

Managing a Message Center. When calls come in, the message is recorded by a staff member and posted under the letter of the receiver's surname. Personnel operating the message center should be told to fold over the message, leaving only the name visible so as to discourage snoopers, and should also be instructed to be polite but firm when dealing with a snooper. The message center is designed to keep office- and home-generated communications open for attendees and to facilitate communication among attendees on-site during the convention. With thousands of people all in the same place, it is difficult to find any one person; having a central message/meeting facility well staffed and efficiently operated will be appreciated by all attendees.

The phone number for the message center should be posted for quick reference by attendees, but more important, the number should appear in all the preshow materials that are mailed to registrants. The best place to post the number is in the show program, which is usually sent to registrants several weeks before opening day.

Public Telephones

Numerous telephones, conveniently placed, should be available throughout the public areas of the convention center—on the exhibit floor, in the hallways of the meeting-room areas, and in the public areas of the main lobby and registration unit. Not all exhibitors have phones installed in their booths, and they should not have to travel great distances to make calls. The same applies to attendees. Although portable phone banks are an expense, you may want to consider installing them in lounge areas on the exhibit floor, as well as in any other area you feel needs them.

Assessing Needs for Public Telephones

If a show is in progress during your initial site inspection, you will be able to assess the adequacy of the telephone areas by watching the floor traffic and telephone access. If you see long lines at the phone stations during the show, you should consider budgeting for additional telephones.

Avoid the potential for long lines at telephones; they cause people to leave the premises in search of a phone. Attendees and exhibitors alike should feel secure when they are away from their homes and offices, and it is the show manager's responsibility to see that people do not have needless stress in contacting their families or co-workers. Short tempers caused by long waiting lines for phones set a negative atmosphere. When long phone lines cause attendees to be late for appointments with exhibitors or to miss a presentation they came to hear, they will be frustrated by what amounts to poor show management of an easily remedied situation. Conversely, you won't have problems getting attendees to return year after year when the family or the boss feels confident that messages will be posted at the message center and that calls can be returned without undue delay.

In-house Telephones

In chapter 4 are outlined the number and types of rooms, exclusive of meeting rooms, that are necessary to the business of the show—accounting, press, office central, and audiovisual storage rooms, among others. Most of these rooms need to have a communications link for contact with other personnel running the show, as well as with the outside. The following list of requirements for telephones represents a communications network that is useful for shows of all sizes and that will ensure that all service centers be able to keep in contact with show management. The number of instruments can, of course, be increased according to individual needs.

Pressroom	2 incoming/outgoing. Use: reporters, pressroom staff.
On-site registration	1 incoming/outgoing. Use: credit-card verification, general communications.
Office central	Minimum of 2, with two lines each, one line being equipped

	with a rotary hunt capability (that is, when one line is busy, the phone will automatically find an available line).
Show manager's office	1 incoming/outgoing.
Exhibitor registration	1 incoming/outgoing. Use: same as for on-site registration.
Exhibit manager's office	1 incoming/outgoing.
Travel company booth	1 incoming/outgoing.
Ground operator booth (airport shuttle, restaurant reservations, and so on)	1 or 2 incoming/outgoing, restricted to local.
Message center	1 or 2, incoming only
Accounting office	1 or 2 incoming/outgoing.

A chart listing all the rooms with phone requirements should be sent to the convention services manager. Attached to the chart should be a floor plan of each room, to facilitate proper placement of the telephones.

8
Working with a Destination Management Company: Managing the Logistics of Large Events

They come bearing different names: ground operators, special events coordinators, meeting and corporate entertainment groups, destination management companies. But whatever their name, you would be hard-pressed to find a convention manager able to conduct a successful show without them.

Different professionals have different talents. You, as a meeting planner, plan the convention, a multifaceted event. You do not dispatch buses or hire the drivers. Nor do you set tables in the banquet hall, blow up balloons, or wash dishes. Obviously, you hire others to do these things. By enlisting the services of a destination management company, you go one step further and hire someone to hire everyone. In other words, a destination management company coordinates your coordination.

When the meeting industry was in its infancy, the services of destination management companies were usually confined to arranging for shuttles, planning spouse events, and perhaps helping to coordinate nonhotel special events. Often these companies were poorly managed, disorganized, and vague about pricing their services. The disorganization did not stem essentially from ignorance or a lack of professionalism but occurred because the companies were trying to meet the needs of a rapidly expanding and equally disorganized industry with little or no experience.

Progress on Both Sides

In the past ten years, amazing progress has been made in both the meeting industry and destination management companies. Companies that began by offering fashion shows and makeup lessons and organizing shopping excursions for the wives of delegates now offer everything from executive-relocation orientation programs for Fortune 500 corporations to unique and grand theme parties developed for tens, hundreds, or thousands of people.

It is important to understand the business of a destination management company, how it makes its money, how to enlist its services, and what the proper expectations and ethics involved in the relationship are.

Even though a party is being held in a hotel, you may still need the services of a destination management company to supply the hotel with props and entertainers and to help the hotel execute the more elaborate theme parties sometimes planned during large conventions. By working with the ground operator directly, you will gain greater control over the quality of the event.

Hiring Staff on a Temporary Basis

When enlisting the services of a destination management company, keep in mind that you are, in a manner of speaking, hiring staff on a temporary basis. Company personnel check the seating arrangements before special dinners; see to the flowers, musicians, and waiters; and will also handle your tipping. They are the ones in the kitchen snooping around and looking into the pots. They greet your guests in your absence and shuttle them safely home.

Special Advantages of Destination Management Companies

Buying Power. Since destination management companies give a great deal of business to local merchants and companies—florists, bus companies, performing artists, special sites for parties—they have buying power. Their bargaining clout and industry discounts should reduce the prices for events and materials that you would not normally be able to negotiate with your onetime-only status. These are the intangibles that a good destination management company brings to the task. These are also the cost savings that a reputable destination management company will pass on to the meeting planner.

Knowledge of Supplier Behavior. A destination management company has knowledge of the behavior of individual suppliers and will use that knowledge to further enhance their services to the meeting planner. Not all suppliers deliver on time, purchase the finest ingredients, or deal fairly with their customers. The final product, the special event, is greatly enriched by this insider's knowledge.

Elimination of the Middleman. Many hotels neither have amassed a storehouse full of props nor wish to get involved in building and storing them. A convention services manager will often call on a ground operator to fulfill a meeting planner's order for decorations and props. Using the destination management company directly eliminates the middleman and can result in substantial savings.

Submitting a Request for a Proposal

The procedures for seeking bids from destination management companies are the same as those for a convention and visitor's bureau in chapter 2 or for a show decorator in chapter 5.

In a request for a proposal to a destination management company, list the number and type of parties you will be giving and the number of anticipated attendees; provide profile of the typical attendee for each party (VIPs, younger people at an earlier stage of their career, and so on); and state either where the event will be held or that you would like suggestions for special sites for it. List the type of entertainment desired, or state that you would like suggestions for entertainment. Detail transportation needs to bring attendees to and from the site, and include budget parameters for each event.

Importance of Submitting Accurate Attendance Figures

If you are planning to have a function at a special site and not at a hotel, an art gallery, or a museum, for instance, it is important to be as accurate as possible when supplying attendance figures. Although it is not a problem to anticipate an increase of 10 percent from the time of planning the event until the actual invitations are mailed, overshooting by hundreds could result in eliminating sites that might be used were the numbers more realistic. It is also difficult for the destination management company to come up with proper cost figures if projections are inaccurate, especially when food-and-beverage items are involved.

All-Inclusive, Cost-per-Head Figure

When requesting a proposal, ask for brief suggestions for each event, including an estimated cost. You may ask for a more in-depth treatment of one special event, with total costs including transportation and the company's fee, presented in a cost-per-person format. Having an all-inclusive, cost-per-person figure is the easiest way to keep within your budget when working with so many variables; it allows specific costs to be easily isolated. If you want to include flowers or exclude special linens, for instance, you can easily get the figures. This method gives you the opportunity to fine-tune your budget.

Management Fees

The destination management company's fees for each event, when delineated in the manner described above, should be quickly and clearly presented. Typically, the fee for a specific event is a percentage of the event's total cost. An event that will cost perhaps $20,000 for site rental, flowers, transportation, food-and-beverage requirements, and decorations will have an administration fee of say, 10 percent added on to the cost. The specific percentage will depend on the complexity of the event and the time involved in the planning. The more information you can give the destination management company before it submits its proposal, the less time will be spent in pursuing unsuitable sites or inappropriate themes.

Charging for Proposals

There has been some talk lately among destination management firms about charging for proposals. This talk is mostly due, I think, to the fact that meeting planners have been known to use the ideas for theme parties suggested by these groups while not employing the particular company that created the concept. These proposals are customized for each client and represent many hours of work and creative thinking. For particularly elaborate affairs, the companies may even write special musical scores for introducing speakers or products. The notion of charging for proposals is a reaction to an unfortunate situation. Although today, if you steal someone else's idea for a special theme party you are probably just earning a bad reputation within the meeting industry, the day may not be far off when you will be hauled into court for doing so. The thoughts expressed in this book are copyrighted, and a ground operator's efforts are entitled to similar protection.

Evaluating Proposals and Checking References

When the proposals arrive, compare costs and ideas, make a tentative decision, and then call the references.

What appears to be a bargain might turn out to be a case of "you get what you pay for." Most meeting planners are happy to share experiences with their colleagues. Heed their advice, but also check with your convention and visitors bureau contact to make sure—as in the case of security reference checks—that any problems were not caused by the meeting planner's failing to do his or her share of the work in submitting a proper request for a proposal with precise information. If the reference seems out of character with your perception of the company or is less than complimentary, it may be worthwhile to check the quality of the reference.

Interviewing the Company. Since the working relationship between a meeting planner and the destination management company representative is essential to your successes, a personality match, confirmed by a face-to-face interview, is most important. Some companies have exclusive access to desirable sites that only they can offer to their clients; others have entire warehouses filled with props amassed over the years, making the cost of theme parties no so expensive as you might think. But if the chemistry is wrong, the relationship just won't work.

Talking with Local Suppliers. In addition to checking references with meeting planners who have worked with the company and to interviewing the company's representative, talk with local suppliers, hotel banquet managers, and the manager at the convention center. These people are neighbors of and quite often friends with your prospective aide-de-camp. They have worked together on many shows, coordinating and helping each other. Listen carefully to what they have to say or not say. A pattern will emerge, and you'll be able to make an informed decision based on fact and feel.

Proposal Etiquette

When you have made your final choice, promptly contact the other destination management companies from whom you have requested proposals and inform them of your decision. They will then be able to release any sites they may be holding in your name.

A Typical Request for a Proposal and a Sample Response to It

The following is an example of a typical specification outline for a request for a proposal.

Event: A reception hosted by the president of an organization.

Day/date/time: Tuesday, June 5, 6:30–8:30 P.M.

Number of expected guests: 200 to 225.

Means of invitation: Special guests of the president; by invitation only.

Site: An elegant private club, art gallery, or museum.

Transportation: Attendees will be scattered among all the hotels on the housing block. Some will be leaving the reception and proceeding to other exhibitor-sponsored events. Drivers and dispatchers should, within reason, be flexible in accommodating drop-off requests.

   A guest list, annotated with the name of the hotel of each guest, will be supplied. Guests will be asked to wear their name tags and to give their invitations to the bus dispatcher before boarding the bus.

Food-and-beverage requirements: Regional specialities. Bar set with premium names. Canapés, finger food, hot and cold.

Entertainment: Please make suggestions. Note that when attendees are given the opportunity to dance, they usually do; however, if the site is more suited to strolling strings or a piano and violin, dancing is not mandatory. If the site can offer opportunities for dancing as well as an area with a more subdued atmosphere, we may be able to include both, given that we have a little flexibility in the budget for this event. In your proposal, please include variations of the theme.

Budget: The total budget proposal for this event should include charges for catering, food-and-beverage requirements, site rental, waiters, bartenders, entertainment, gratuities, flowers, and all incidentals, as well as transportation and your fee. Our budget cannot exceed $17,000.

As a result of the above request for a proposal, the following sample response for suggested theme parties was received. In this case, the ground operator preparing the proposal was The Capital Informer of Washington, D.C.

> *Event:* President's reception.
> *Place:* The Phillips Collection.
> *Date:* Tuesday, June 5.
> *Time:* 6:30–8:30 P.M.
>
> In 1921, Marjorie and Duncan Phillips opened to the public their home in the exclusive Dupont Circle area of Washington, D.C. On the walls were paintings by Chardin, Monet, Twachtman, Whistler,and Hassam. This was the beginning of the Phillips Collection, the first museum of modern art in the United States. The gracious gallery rooms of this private museum provide an intimate setting for presenting this extraordinary collection of postimpressionistic and modern art. The highlight of the museum's installation is *The Luncheon of the Boating Party* (1881), by Pierre-Auguste Renoir. This magnificent painting is considered a masterpiece and will create an elegant atmosphere for your special visit to the Phillips Collection.
>
> Guests will arrive by bus at the main entrance to the Phillips Collection, on Twenty-first Street. Capital Informer hostesses will welcome them on the street and direct them to the party rooms. Should your organization require a receiving line, one will be arranged to take place in the center foyer. As guests enter, they will also be greeted by a three-piece strolling strings ensemble that will be located on the staircase. This group will play throughout the reception, on both floors of the gallery. To the right of the center hall is a parlor, followed by the Music Room, that will feature one of the three bars placed throughout the gallery space on both floors. All food stations will be located on the first floor, as dictated by the rules of the Phillips Collection; however, waiters will pass hors d'oeuvres on the second floor.
>
> *Theme 1*
>
> The Music Room will be decorated for a Victorian summer garden party. Bright-peach-colored skirting accented by crisp white organdy overlays will decorate the food stations placed in the center of the room. White baskets filled with potted peach-colored geraniums in full bloom will complete the very elegant yet comfortable look. Floral displays of fresh-cut salmon and white flowers will also be used, as will an accent color of periwinkle blue to signify your association's logo color. A large bouquet of white lilacs will grace another first-floor reception room. The floral selections have been chosen to lighten the feeling of the dark, heavily paneled walls and are in keeping with the floral displays typical of this turn-of-the-century residence. Throughout

the reception, guests will enjoy a medley of American piano music played on the grand piano located in the Music Room.

Theme 2

In keeping with the oriental influence as captured in the many impressionistic paintings throughout the collection, The Capital Informer has chosen to carry this theme throughout the food display and decorations. Round tables will feature melon-colored damask cloths with black cocktail napkins and a simple white china pattern. Food will be displayed in oriental baskets and Imari bowls and platters, and floral decorations will also feature the traditional ikebana design. Fans, too, will be included in the decorations.

The same menu is recommended for both party themes. The food stations will include two centers of activity inclusive of a carving station and a raw bar. The menu below provides a complete listing of food service.

Bars will be complete with name-brand liquor, beer, and wine.

Guests will be encouraged to browse throughout the entire gallery. Docents will be stationed throughout the house to answer any and all questions concerning the collection. Please refer to the list of highlights in the collection. We have found that this information, when known ahead of time, makes the visit far more valuable.

In case of inclement weather, The Capital Informer will make provisions for limited use of oversize umbrellas. A permanent coatroom is located on the first floor of the gallery. At this time no personnel have been budgeted for this service, as we feel that even if it is raining, there will be limited need for the service.

MENU FOR PRESIDENT'S RECEPTION

Savories to be Passed
Tiny Crab Cakes on Brioche Toasts,
Topped with Capered Tartar
English Sausage Rolls
Warm Cheddar-and-Bacon Melts

Mariners Raw Bar
Plump Chincoteque Oysters
and Sweet Littleneck Clams,
Served with Tangy Red Sauce
Freshly Grated Horseradish
Lemon Wedges
Tabasco

Oyster Crackers
Gingered Shrimp with Chinese Cucumber

Butlers Rib Room
Standing Ribs of Prime Beef Rubbed with Fresh Herbs,
Carved to Order, and Served with Horseradish Cream and
Bernaise Sauce,
Silver Bowls of Rye, Pumpernickel, and Seeded Rolls

The Queen's Table
Ribbon Sandwiches of Ham, Pistachios, Asparagus, and Sautéed
Mushrooms with Wheat Bread and Herbed Cheese
Raisin and Candied Orange Scones Plumped with Smoked
Turkey and Watercress Mayonnaise
Nutmeat Pâté—Pistachios, Walnuts, and Gruyère,
Condensed to Make a Wonderful Heart-shaped Pâté
French Bread Slices, Watercress Rolls
Seedless Green Grapes Rolled in Cream Cheese and Nuts
Mousse of Black-fin Crab and Shrimp,
Served with Pumpernickel Rounds

Brie Layered with Tropical Fruits
Marscapone Cheese Layered in Grape Leaves
Saga Blue Cheese
Bath Oliver Crackers, Pumpernickel Flat Breads
Charming Multicolored Baskets of Snow Peas, Baby Carrots,
Asparagus Tips, and Yellow and Red Pepper with Bouquets of
Carved Vegetables, to Include Carrot Rosebuds, Red Radish
Blossoms, Turnip Camelias, Cabbage Lilies, and White Radish
Sprays, Country Curd and Herb Dip

Jumbo Strawberries with Devonshire Cream
Chocolate Lace Cookies
Victoria Tartlets Topped with Candied Violets
Lemon Curd Tartlets
French Roast Coffee with Cream and Sugar
English Tea[a]

[a]Reproduced with permission of The Capital Informer, Washington, D.C.

I toured the Phillips Collection, as well as several other sites, one year before the event. This property and several others were available. I chose the Phillips, and after I made my decision, this proposal was developed. The cost per head was figured to the penny and was exactly what appeared on the final bill. The party was a huge success—though with that menu and environment, the guests would have had to work hard to make it a failure. My contact at The Capital Informer was the first one to call me on the morning of the event, and we were in constant contact throughout the day. She saw the last guest out the door and onto the bus, and one of her staff members drove one of our guests back to the hotel because he had missed the bus.

A Toronto Fantasy

A similar set of specifications was submitted to Coordination Plus, a destination management company in Toronto, with the following results.

Medieval Fantasy at Casa Loma

One of Ontario's most colorful residents during the early 1900s was the entrepreneur and staunch royalist Sir Henry Pellat. This evening, participants will be guests at his extravagant "medieval-style" castle, Casa Loma.

Upon entering the castle, you will have an opportunity to get to know more about its fascinating creator, as you wander from room to room noting the modern inventions of his time that have become today's antiques. With no expense spared, Casa Loma was truly one of the most stately homes in North America and a fitting place to entertain Sir Henry's royal friends in the manner to which they were accustomed in Europe.

There will be two large buffet areas (one in the Library and one along Peacock Alley). In addition, bars will be set up in the Great Hall and the Library.

Trumpeters in uniform will herald and great the guests as they step off the buses.

Costumed wenches will offer tidbits and wine as the guests enter the castle and will circulate throughout the evening offering morsels as part of the overall themed environment.

Wandering minstrels, jugglers in jester costumes, and a magician will entertain guests as they roam through the various rooms of the castle.

> An exhibit of replicas of crown jewels, guarded by a fully cos-
> tumed beefeater, will be in main hall. The beefeater will explain the
> significance of each gem an doffer amusing anecdotes.
>
> A photographer will be available to snap shots of guests with the
> beefeater, jesters, wenches, minstrels, and jugglers.
>
> Floral decorations of the era will be placed on buffet tables, in the
> ladies' washroom, and at the main entrance.[a]

[a]Reproduced with permission of Coordination Plus, Toronto, Canada.

As you can see, a great deal of time and creative energy goes into these
proposals. They are presented with pride and enthusiasm, with the hope that
you will contract with the company in question.

Developing and Planning Spouse Tours

A complete request for a proposal should include your requirements for spouse
tours. When compiling a specification sheet for such tours, include the
following:

- Description of the group (salespeople, booksellers, cowboys or cowgirls,
  rocket scientists, and so on).

- Figures from previous tours for the past two or three years—that is, the
  total number of tours, number and type of cancellations, and how many
  tours exceeded attendance expectations. Copies of the printed material for
  past tours are helpful to tour designers. Moreover, past tours' pricing will
  serve as a guideline for your group's price range.

Customized Planning

Spouse tours developed by a destination management company are not cookie-
cutter affairs, pulled out of the file when your group comes to town. Each tour
is created to appeal to your group's type, taste, pocketbook, and interests. Some
people are just not going to be happy touring museums and art galleries all day
and would rather spend an afternoon bargain hunting and seeing the city or bird-
watching or exploring the countryside.

Importance of Arrival/Departure Patterns

Whether attendees are more likely to arrive at the site on the weekend before the convention to tour the city or are more likely to stay a week after the show to do so will affect the timing of your tours. If the destination is a likely departure point for a vacation, your pattern could change as well. A convention held in San Francisco in the spring or summer or in Orlando in the winter could provoke a change in arrival/departure patterns. The best you can do is make an educated guess and use past data as an indicator of your group's needs.

Finalizing the Arrangements

When reviewing the proposal for spouse tours with the destination management company, make sure that all the terms for purchasing and distributing the tickets are clearly stated. Most destination management companies do not mail tickets to attendees. Typically, the meeting planner supplies the company with a booth in the convention center or a tabletop area in the headquarters hotel for distributing tour tickets. If the tours begin before the opening day of the show, make sure that the destination management company has made arrangements to deliver tickets to attendees when they register at their hotels.

Information sent to delegates about tours should include a return coupon that is addressed directly to the tour operators. The meeting planner does not get involved after the initial mailing of the informational brochure.

Insurance

A final addition to your request for a proposal from a destination management company should be for verification of liability insurance coverage for tours, as well as proof of insurance from the bus company that will be supplying buses for the tours and shuttle service.

All sites that will be used for special events planned by the destination management company should also show evidence of proper insurance coverage.

Managing Big Events

Managing a party of two to three thousand attendees is less complicated and daunting than one might expect. Reducing the event to several components is the simplest plan of attack for bringing it under control. Such subdivision is approached as follows, with this hypothetical group profile:

Event: A party honoring the volunteers and members of an organization. This group represents the next wave in the organization's leadership.

Profile of participants: Up-and-coming young professionals between the ages of twenty-four and thirty-five. The lower age of the spectrum is more heavily represented. There will also be more singles than married couples.

Site: Hotel ballroom.

Time: 8:00–11:00 P.M.

Means of invitation: Announcement in all meeting promotional pieces; on-site announcements. This is a yearly event, open to all comers presenting a registration badge.

Room setup: If the room has a built-in stage, the dance floor would be placed immediately in front of it. Beyond the dance floor, it is best, with a crowd of this size, to leave a wide area onto which bodies can overflow. It is also desirable to have in the room as many large round tables, with chairs, as the room can hold. The dance floor in many hotels is a flexible arrangement of 3-foot wooden squares and can be ordered as large or as small as necessary. If the expected attendance is twenty-five hundred people, estimate how many might be on the dance floor at any one time. For this group, 60 percent is a reasonable guess; the balance of the party will be either sitting or standing in line for drinks. Multiply the expected attendance figure by 60 percent and you get fifteen hundred dancing people. Multiply that figure by three and you'll find that you need 4,500 square feet of dance floor.

Beyond the tables should be adequate space for standing, as well as space for people to line up at the bars.

If the room does not have a stage, one will have to be built. The hotel staff is the most knowledgeable about stage placement, but it is a good rule to have the stage on the wall opposite the entrance doors, if this is the wall that runs the width of the room—the longest wall. Placing the band at the narrow end will cause a tunnel effect, and the people at the back of the room won't be able to see the stage very well and will feel somewhat left out.

Bars

Ideally, you will want to eliminate crowding and long lines at the bars. And unless your organization is extremely well heeled and can offer a hosted bar wherein attendees approach the bar, place an order, and get a drink, you will have a cash-bar setup. Cash bars take a bit longer to process people: Money exchanges hands at a cashier's table, and drink tickets are distributed, to be cashed in at a bar set up in another part of the function room.

Cash versus Hosted Bars

When you are dealing with groups of this size, it is important—for avoiding bankruptcy courts—to know the difference between a cash and a hosted bar.

A meeting planner of my acquaintance learned the distinction between a cash bar and a hosted bar at a reception for approximately fifteen hundred people, when he saw no money changing hands. Although he picked up on the situation within the first few minutes of the party and immediately took steps to stop the flow of free liquor, $2,000 worth of drinks had been consumed by the amazed but delighted crowd. Apparently the meeting planner, who was new to the industry, was unfamiliar with the term *hosted,* and when asked if the bar would be hosted he haughtily replied, "Of course"—in his mind thinking, I'm not going to allow fifteen hundred people to mix their own drinks.

Avoiding Long Lines

The object of efficient planning for crowds and bar needs is to have (a) enough bars to handle the initial rush to the bars without too much crowding but (b) not so many bars that they line the walls of the ballroom and the bartenders sit idly after the first rush for drinks. With a group of this size, most food-and-beverage managers will waive the cost of bartenders and cashiers; nevertheless, having too many bartenders still costs someone money, and it's not going to be the hotel. Therefore, try to work with the food-and-beverage manager for an equitable distribution of labor. (The industry standard is one bartender per hundred persons at a function of this type.)

Cashier Stations

The cash-bar setup will also include cashier stations, located away from the bars. The cashiers will have their own line for attendees to buy drink tickets (These tickets are sold at a price determined prior to the event, during contract negotiations.) Attendees purchase tickets and then walk over to the bar and exchange their tickets for the drinks of their choosing.

Wine-and-Beer-Only Bars

If you know your group's personality and have information from previous events to give you an accurate count of drink tickets sold for wine, beer, and mixed drinks, you may find that the purchases run more to wine and beer than to mixed drinks or vice versa. In any case, if an obvious pattern appears, wine-and-beer-only bars and cashier lines can be set up, with appropriate signs alerting everyone to this scheme, along with regular bars that dispense everything, including wine and beer. Since wine and beer are faster to serve, this arrangement helps to stay ahead of the long lines. Unless your group drinks faster than bartenders can pour, with this format you should not experience tremendous problems with long lines and complaining guests.

It has been my experience with this type of group that after the first few rounds of drinks and with a good band, no one seems to mind standing in line. The exception is the meeting planner (who is preoccupied with the people standing in line), who would perhaps be better served by getting in line and buying his or her own drink ticket.

The Need for Hotels to Keep Accurate Counts

Even though the organization is not paying for liquor in a cash bar arrangement many meeting planners write into their contract a clause stating that food-and-beverage usage must be clearly and accurately accounted for at cash events, and submitted in a timely fashion. Although often reluctant, for whatever reason, to part with this information, food-and-beverage managers should be strongly urged to cooperate. Such information can only improve the meeting planner's performance and, in turn, make for more professional behavior on the part of the next food-and-beverage manager working on the party the following year.

Crowd Control and Group Behavior Patterns

A phenomenon I have observed with a group of people of this size (numbering in the thousands) who have been to meetings together all day—and sometimes for several days—is that they tend to set up their own game rules at these affairs. After having managed all the preliminaries, one lone meeting planner is no match for this group, and unless you have specific events planned throughout the night—awards, games, and so forth—you can't do much else but just sit back and let it happen.

Should you find that raucousness is reaching an unruly pitch, have the banquet manager close up all but two bars and slowly raise the lights. Bright lights have the same effect as tossing cold water on a rowdy group and is far less controversial than using the fire hoses.

Arrivals and Departures

So far, this section has discussed the actual party with everyone drinking and dancing. Although the party itself is of paramount importance, orchestrating the orderly welcome and timely departure of your guests is not to be overlooked. The following paragraphs introduce some methods designed to meet this challenge.

Planning a Reception Area for Ticketed Events

Many parties of this size are either *ticketed events*—that is, everyone must present a ticket or a registration badge to gain admittance to the site—or events at which an organization will buy the first drink for attendees and then distribute tickets to them as the guests enter the ballroom. Sometimes both procedures are used for a single event.

Setting up the reception area for an event of this size is a major part of your plan and figures greatly in how traffic is controlled.

Most ballrooms are entered through what is called a prefunction area: a large area immediately outside the ballroom doors. Ideally, the ballroom is not on the same floor as the lobby area. Such isolation of the ballroom keeps gate-crashers at a minimum. Moreover, if all the attendees are arriving by shuttle bus, the farther away the ballroom is from the entrance, the more widely dispersed will the crowds become, riding escalators and elevators; this situation tends to serve as an automatic traffic-flow regulator. Tables in the prefunction area should be set perpendicular to the entrance, thereby becoming the rough equivalent of cattle chutes to separate the herds into workable numbers for facilitating badge checking. If you, like some other meeting planners, have enough money in your budget to buy the first one or two drinks for your group, this is the place to hand out the tickets. Although it's ideal to staff these tables with your own personnel, you may have to hire temporary help to manage the first wave of arrivals.

Security

It is a good idea to have one strolling plainclothes guard for an event of this type to keep an eye on the other doors that lead into the ballroom. Although entrances to these large rooms are equipped with *crash doors*—that is, doors that can be opened from the inside by pushing on bars and that can be locked on the outside (like the doors in movie theaters)—people leaving by these side doors could open the way to the uninvited. In addition, many fire laws prohibit the locking of these doors from either side.

Shuttle Busing for Guests

In handling parties of this size, it is important to have shuttle buses available at all times. Depending on your hotel distribution in relation to the party site, during the active hours of the party you may need only a few buses to drop off people who leave the party early. Most buses are hired for a four-hour minimum, an efficient way to make use of them. Be prepared, however, to have the buses run later than expected. Don't think that just because it is now 10:30 P.M. and your printed matter and signs state that the party ends at 11:00, your group will now dutifully begin to file out.

Go Home!

When a party is going well and the band is particularly good, it is not unusual for party goers to take up a collection and bribe the band to play for another hour. If you know that this scenario has occurred in the past, communicating with the band ahead of time about your wishes and about adherence to the schedule is mandatory. If, however, you see that everyone is having a good time, your budget allows for a little extension of the bus service, and you don't want to be drawn and quartered, now is the time to be flexible.

As you can see, planning for this type of party begins well in advance—at the time of the site inspection. Of course, you can't pick a property based solely on one event; many conventions have two or three events, with various group profiles. You may also have a more staid group of attendees, primarily older couples, who should not (though there is always the exception) pose so many problems as the group in the above example. I have merely given you a worst-case scenario so as to outline suggested solutions.

The Band

Naturally, everyone judges the success of a party by his or her own expectations. The young single person wants to have a wide range of dance partners, a great band, and a chance to get away from it all for a night, among other things. In this attendee's mind, the possibilities are endless. The food-and-beverage manager would like everyone to drink to excess but not get drunk and ruin the rug. The upwardly mobile couple would like to meet the movers and shakers of the organization and make important contacts. The band hopes that its music will whip everyone into a frenzy, that one of your guests is really a record producer. But in reality, the band knows it must follow your dictates, and decorum should, if not reign, at least be waiting in the wings. Therefore, make sure that the band understands that when you think it is time for something slow and mellow, you get it. If you don't want band members taking requests from attendees, make sure they stick to their repertoire. Find out if they have the stamina to go that extra hour in advance of the party. If they don't you won't have to plan for bus overtime for the shuttles.

Auditioning Bands for Special Events

My greatest successes with bands I have hired have come through the destination management company, because over the years it has seen the local talent in action and is assured of that talent's professionalism. Like you, the members of the band want to perform at their best; give them the opportunity. Don't set out hard-and-fast rules, and don't forget praise, backed up by a monetary gift. These are creative people, and a duly noted appreciation of their talents can inspire a more exciting performance.

Handling Breaks

Some bands arrange for music to be taped and played during their breaks; others do not. Make sure that someone has something to play to keep the momentum going when the band is taking a break. In addition, make clear to band members whether or not they are to avail themselves, during breaks, of the food and beverages set out for guests. If the band is quite large, its members could interfere with your guests having access to the tables.

Paying for Overtime

When calculating the length of the party, it is always best to anticipate the maximum length of time that the band will play. If the band is requested to play longer than the contracted time, the additional time will usually be billed at overtime rates.

A Strategy Regarding Signs

Using signs creatively—or rather, creatively *not* using signs—is a technique whose adoption will depend on the group. Just as the distance from the hotel entrance to the ballroom and the number of elevators or escalators needed to reach the party have an effect on traffic flow, so do signs or a lack of them.

All hotels have signboards placed in the lobbies to announce group functions and the various rooms where each function is being held. You can just stop there, letting guests find the hotel floor plan (which is usually nowhere near the signs) and locate the ballroom on their own—a method by which you can creatively "lose" perhaps one entire busload of party goers out of four or five busloads that are arriving simultaneously. This approach helps check the flow of traffic during that crucial opening hour of your party. Just be ready to accept complaints that you will receive when the "lost" attendees finally get to the ballroom. It will be no different in amount or kind than the abuse you will receive when they have to stand in line to have their badges checked. People seem to get particularly upset when they can hear the band playing and see the people inside already dancing. Choose your poison.

This strategy will usually limit the waiting in line and, if you have absolutely no scruples, can be blamed on the hotel by saying that it lost the directional signs you so carefully created. The method is especially helpful if your ground operator, whom you know to be a stickler for detail, is preoccupied with getting all guests to the hotel exactly on time in order to enjoy the sight of four or five buses disgorging hundreds of party goers all at once. It's better to let the ground operator and dispatchers do their job, while you quietly handle the traffic flow in your own way.

Sometimes meeting planners become overly concerned with what is a logistics problem that does not lend itself to a satisfactory solution. It is best to remember that the overwhelming majority of attendees are reasonable individuals who can size up the problems of moving large numbers of people.

Be warned, however, that a lack of signs works only for a group with this particular profile between the ages of 24 and 35. If you are having a formal affair, I wouldn't suggest employing this method. Signs clearly pointing the way to the function should naturally, be used in that case.

In concluding this chapter on destination management companies and the management of big events, it seems appropriate to take note of the particular characteristics these companies have in common, wherever I have staged a convention. That characteristic is creativity, and it serves as a reminder that this industry does allow a great deal of personality to emerge on the part of meeting planners as well as hotel and destination company managers. Hence, readers are here reminded to enjoy the opportunity and not let their responsibilities outweigh their imagination.

9
Registration: Developing an Efficient Registration Area

The nightmare of every meeting planner and every convention attendee is long registration lines. When the doors open on the first day of the show, it seems that all the shuttle buses that you painstakingly scheduled do indeed appear on time. Congratulations—now attendees are all coming in the door at the same time and it is up to you to register them quickly and efficiently.

Calculating registration space and then furnishing it to accommodate thousands of people efficiently are not so difficult if you break down the entire registration process into manageable sections. For the purposes of this chapter, let us base our calculations on a convention that attracts approximately five thousand professional attendees, fifteen hundred exhibitors, and five hundred more people composing spouses and guests.

Defining Registrants by Type

Typically, shows have two types of registrants: (a) preregistrants, who have registered by mail before their arrival at the show, and (b) on-site registrants, who have waited to come to the show to register. Your plans must be able to efficiently process both types of registrants. In this, how you lay out the registration area in the lobby of the convention center will be key.

Registration Procedures

Both types of registrants should be processed in the same area; however, different sections of the area should be set aside and equipped in entirely different ways.

The process involving preregistered individuals is greatly simplified because all the paperwork has been done beforehand—the registration form filled out, a check or credit-card information included with the form, and the form mailed to the registrar. In turn, the registrar has processed the check, created a name badge, and mailed a receipt and confirmation to the registrant. Arriving on site, the preregistered attendee merely steps up to whichever desk is designated with the letter of his or her last name, presents the receipt, and picks up the name badge and any registration materials—printed program, special announcements, and so on.

The on-site registration process, in contrast, takes a bit longer. The delegate must first pick up a registration form, fill it out, make out a check, and then stand in a cashier line. Next, the cashier reviews the information, checks that the amount of the check is correct, and signs off on the registration form. The registrant then proceeds to the registration desk, submits the receipt, and waits for the clerk to prepare a badge.

A registration area of 10,000 square feet in the lobby of a convention center will adequately handle a crowd of this size.

Using the Hollow Square Configuration
for Greater Efficiency

The configuration of the registration area is a factor in planning for expedient registration. A long row of desks, stretching a block in length, is not so desirable as a large square area or a well-proportioned rectangle. Setting up your registration area within a hollow square will allow your staff to circulate freely from one part of the area to another without traversing long distances.

Efficiency is at its peak when everyone can see the area in one sweep of the eye. The person who has been assigned to the preregistration area can, with no attendees lining up, quickly scan the area, see instantly where help is needed, and move quickly to assist in that area. With a linear configuration, this advantage would not be possible.

An additional factor in utilizing the hollow square is the amount of storage space made available in the center of the square. Setting skirted tables in the center of the square gives you not only storage space under the tables with easy access to registration materials but a great deal more tabletop space to keep materials, credit-card machines, phones, and stationery supplies.

The floor plan below illustrates the layout.

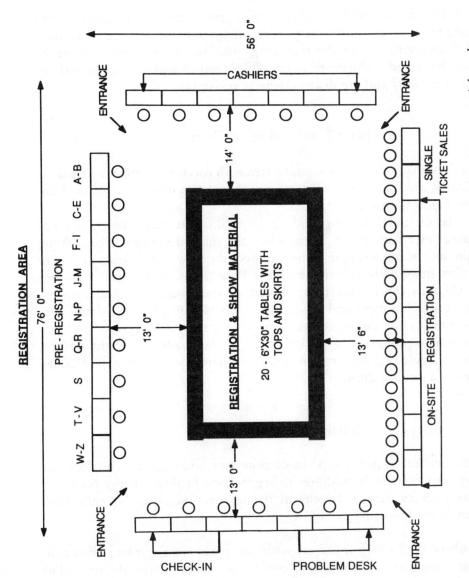

Figure 9–1. *Floor plan of registration area set for convenient access to materials and increased staff efficiency.* Reprinted with permission of Larry Rowell

Using Bank Mazes to Expedite On-site Registration

The standard bank maze with stanchions and ropes is the most efficient way to separate and move people in on site registration lines. Bank lines are psychologically less daunting to the standee than long, snaking lines in front of a row of registration desks and cashiers. Free-form lines tend to add a disorganized appearance to the lobby and are discouraging to registrants.

Floor Plans and Flow Chart

Drawing a floor plan of your registration area with specific, detailed instructions for each booth, area, and aisle is the most useful way to inform the show decorator of the registration area setup.

For ease of understanding and ready facilitation, the written account should appear as a flow chart. Then, when the show decorator is calculating labor requirements, it is a simple matter to check the flow chart, compare it with the floor plan (marked to coincide with the flow chart), and map out a labor schedule. The flow chart you prepare should not only include general information about booth placement and decoration (such as signs), but also detail electrical requirements for the registration area—electricity for registration computers and badge printers and to light signs in the headers over the booths. Below is an example of a registration area flow chart that can easily be adapted for a larger or a smaller show.

Attendee Service Booths

The registration area is also the point of communication for all attendees and the hosting organization. In addition to registration facilities, many organizations create attendee service booths in the registration area. Typically such booths include the following:

- *Membership.* To help members with any problems regarding change of address, missing publications, or confusion over the status of dues and/or to enlist new members.

- *Information (association or organization).* To direct attendees to appropriate personnel—staff in the membership or publications booth, the program chair, the show manager, and so forth.

- *Message center.* Used either by on-site attendees to contact other attendees at the show or for phone messages for attendees from their families or employers. (Information on how to set up a message center appears in chapter 7.)

- *Tour desk.* Usually staffed by the destination management company to handle not only the tours that have been developed for attendees but also restaurant reservations and general requests for information about the city.

- *Car-rental booth.* Staffed free of charge by national or local auto-rental companies as a convenience for attendees. In most cases, the meeting planner, in advance of the show, negotiates the terms of rental rates and advertises the service in materials sent to prospective attendees.

- *Next-year's meeting booth.* Staffed by a representative from the convention and visitors bureau of the city where the next show will be held.

With respect to the last item, most large convention and visitors bureaus have money in their budgets to send a representative to staff a booth in order to greet members and hand out posters, tote bags, pins, and promotional literature. This arrangement adds a festive quality to the registration area, and the giveaways are always fun. Moreover, it gives attendees information about your next show, encouraging them to plan for the next event. Thus, even before your promotional pieces are mailed you have an enthusiastic, knowledgeable person selling the city for you and presenting it in its best light. Working together this way ensures that the city and your organization will have a good turnout next year.

Exhibitor Services: The Exhibitor Lead List

When an attendee registers, he or she is given a name badge listing his or her name, affiliation and home city and state. The badge is also numbered, and when the attendee visits a booth, the salesperson notes the number. At the end of the day, the list of numbers is turned in to the registration personnel and converted to a list that specifies each person's name, company, address, and phone number. The next morning, the exhibitors pick up their lists and fax or mail them to their companies with notations and instructions for follow-up. Many companies have a marketing plan already in place, just waiting for the arrival of these lists. Staff are instructed to verify leads and to mail out requested material so that it is on the potential client's desk when he or she returns from the convention.

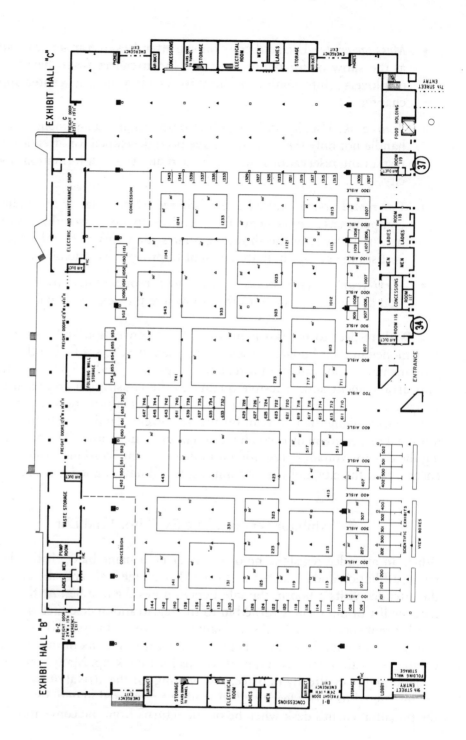

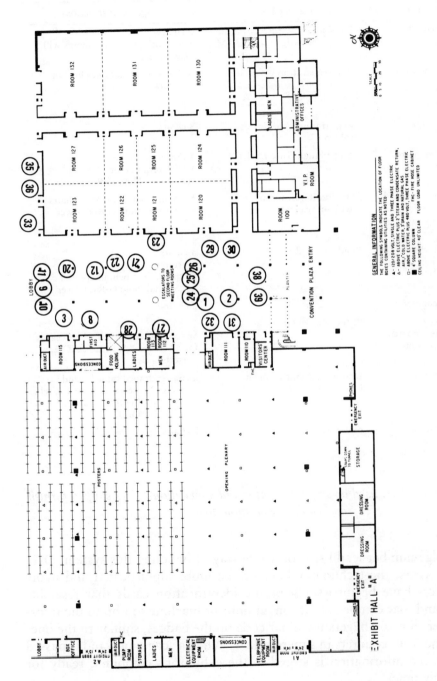

Figure 9–2. *Registration area with placement of service booths numbered to coincide with registration-area flow chart*

Location	Format	Header/Sign	Special Instructions
1, 2	2 counters	"Exhibitor/Guest Registration" × 2 (letter designations: A–M, N–Z)	2 chairs 2 bulletin typewriters/temps will bring own
3, 4, 5, 6, 7, 8	9 counters	"Pre-Registration" × 9 (letter designations: A–B, C–E, F–I, J–M, N–P, Q–R, S, T–V, W–Z)	9 chairs. Draped tables behind counters
9, 10	3 counters	"Registration Questions/ Problems"	3 chairs
11	3 counters	"Typist/Single Ticket Sales"	4 chairs 1 CRT terminal on rear table See Special Note H-Re: power
12, 13, 14, 15, 16, 17, 18, 19, 20	6 counters DE 7 cashier counters	"On-Site Registration" × 5 CRT's on rear table	Maze in front of cashiers chairs See Special Note G-Re: power
21, 22	2 counter height tables (6')	"Badges" × 2	3 chairs 2 printers Draped tables behind counter See Special Note G-Re: power
23	1 counter	"Information"	2 chairs
24	2–4 × 8' posterboards & 1 counter	"Message Center"	2 chairs Special Note: Use our 4" × 4" cards for all letters "A, B, C . . . Z" for posterboards
25	1 booth	Destination Management Company Booth	2 chairs; draped table behind 4 easels (2 easels in booth; 1 easel at Convention Center entrance; 1 easel at back entrance)
26	Built-in, lefthand side facing hall	rent-a-car	2 chairs

Figure 9–3. *Flow chart used by show decorator and convention-center staff to furnish and equip registration area*

The badge-number lead list is only one way of handling this system. Over the past few years, the technology has become more sophisticated and many show managers have begun issuing plastic identification cards that resemble credit cards and that can be run off on an imprint machine to obtain the information. Other show managers use a bar code on the badges, similar to the ones used at the checkout counters in supermarkets. When a scanning wand is passed over the bar, the information is stored in the exhibitor's computer, ready for retrieval at any time.

Location	Format	Header/Sign	Special Instructions
27	1 table	next year's meeting booth	Draped table and 8′ posterboard
28	1 table	special event table	
29, 30	2 counters	membership promotion	modular design—see attached
31, 32	2 counters	"Audio Tapes"	2 chairs; two 8′ draped tables behind
33	20′ linear modular display unit	"Publications Booth"	modular design—see attached
34	4 poster boards	"Announcements" × 4 on 14″ × 22″ stock mounted on the posterboards	two 8′ tables draped in front of boards for handouts
35	2 booths	ancillary group booth	information sent separately
36	(1) 10′ × 10′	fund-raising booth	1 chair; 8′ posterboard; draped table in back
37	2 booths	association chapters	2 draped tables behind; 5 chairs 3 easels; wastebasket
38	1 booth	airport transfer tickets booth	1 draped table, 4 chairs; 1 wastebasket
39	1 table	hospitality booth	1 draped table; 2 chairs; 1 wastebasket; 1 easel; 1 bulletin/posterboard

Special Notes:
A. Provide electrical as necessary for headers
B. A small wastebasket for each counter
C. Apply complimentary 240 square yard carpet allotment to exhibit hall
D. Allow 6′ between registration counters and rear tables
E. Provide 4 × 20 amp, 110-volt dedicated lines under rear tables behind 11, 12, 13, 14, and 15
F. Provide writing counters in front of "On-Site Registration"
G. Draped work tables are required behind all work stations

Figure 9–3. *continued*

Services to Facilitate Attendee Departure

Return Ticket Sales

Last-day departures can be handled quite easily by setting up a return ticket sales booth. There are two ways the sales can be managed and the departures organized.

1. Working with a bus company that services the airport-to-city route, notify the company well in advance (at least eight months to a year) that your group is coming to town. Arrange with the bus company to

staff a booth to sell return tickets for transportation from the convention center to the airport. Your arrangements should specify that the bus company is to develop a customized schedule for your attendees, to accommodate all departures beginning on the days you indicate. This method works for both you and the bus company: Your group doesn't have to worry about getting to the airport, and the bus company, by preselling tickets, knows exactly how many buses it will need and at what times during the show it will need them.

2. Alternatively work with a destination management company to accompany the same purpose. Here, the procedure is the same in providing presale of return tickets. The association will not be charged for this service, the profits being realized through the sale of tickets.

This service is a relatively inexpensive and simple way to enhance attendee satisfaction with the entire convention.

Coat-and-Baggage Checking

For every action, there is an equal and opposite reaction. If you are instituting this master plan to get everyone out of the convention center and to the airport in a timely and convenient manner, you must also plan to get everyone's luggage out of the convention center in a timely and convenient manner. The point of a last-day departure plan is attendee convenience, so that people can check out of their hotels, bring their bags with them to the convention center, and leave from the convention center to the airport.

Attendees won't be too happy if they have to carry their bags around with them all day to avail themselves of the last-day departure plan. Therefore, you must remember to back up your departure plan with an arrangement for storing people's luggage. This task is simply a matter of assigning an area or meeting room large enough to hold the luggage for your group.

Working with your security company, arrange for one or two guards to be posted to the entrance of the room or roped-off area. These guards should be supplied with a large roll of tickets—the type used for raffles, with two tickets joined together with identical numbers. For each bag, the guards should issue a ticket, taping one ticket to the bag and giving the duplicate ticket to the bag's owner. When attendees return to claim their bags, the guards should allow them to enter the room and find their own bags. On their way out, the guards should then check the numbers against the tags taped to the bag.

If the room is not large, you can set up tables, stacked one on top of another, to provide more storage space. This system will probably require another person to get the bags and bring them to the owner, however, which can really slow things up unless you have someone there to store the bags in some kind of logical order. It's always good to have an extra person or two around to keep order in the room if you are using the store-it-yourself method. When people bring their own bags into the room, they will naturally put them in what they view as the most convenient spot—perhaps near the door or on top of other bags. (The poor soul with his or her bags thus smothered may need some help uncovering them.) If you use the stacked-table method for storage, doing so will greatly increase the surface area of storage space and keep the bags in order. If you have a room with two or more doors, people can enter through one door and exit through another, where the exit guard is posted. People carrying bags need room to move, and if they can exit from another doorway, your traffic problems will be simplified.

However you choose to set up your baggage-check area, make sure that this information is included on the flow chart. Convention services must know about the baggage area, even if you are planning only to cordon off space in the registration lobby. Your show decorator also needs to know whether stanchions and cords to rope off the area are required. If you will be using a meeting room for storing bags and it was previously used for an educational session, the audiovisual supervisor needs to know that he or she will have to strike (dismantle) the room in time for convention services to get in to reset it with tables.

Keep in mind that however successful and smooth the show may turn out to be, attendees will always remember their departure if it is harried and fraught with inconvenience. In the days of vaudeville, the trick was to always leave them laughing. In convention management, the trick is to always have them leave with the feeling that attending your show was effortless, fun, educational, and something they want to experience again next year.

10
See No Evil, Hear No Evil: Planning for Perfect Audiovisual Presentations

M any professional associations offer educational programs during a trade show. It is not unusual for a major technical, scientific, or medical program to have hundreds of such presentations, featuring hundreds of speakers. These programs are presented orally and enhanced by slide or video displays. Attendance at them can be quite large, and with a very large trade show that attracts thousands of delegates, often one or several meeting rooms will be set up to accommodate thousands of people. The audiovisual equipment used in these meeting rooms are frequently larger than what one normally sees in local movie theaters.

Overview of a Typical Educational Program

It is crucial that the planning, equipping, staging, and managing of this type of production be as precise as possible.

It is not unlikely that a major educational program that runs for four or five days will have five hundred or more speakers making technical presentations. Medical and technical programs are the most difficult to produce in terms of audiovisuals. The presentations are highly technical; projection and sound must be of excellent quality for maximum understanding of the subject. Many years of research and great expense have gone into the work that is being presented. All this information is condensed into an abstracted form and usually presented in a ten- to twelve-minute time frame, with a five-minute question-and-answer period. Typically, such a show will easily present twenty-four of these *abstracts,* or scientific papers, per day in each meeting room. Using 9 meeting rooms with 24 speakers equals 216 speakers per day, which, times 5 days, equals 1,080 presentations.

Scheduling and Timing of an Educational Program

For the sake of simplicity, assume that the show we are discussing will have the following profile:

- Nine concurrent sessions, each presenting six speakers, in nine meeting rooms.

- Four sessions per day and five days of sessions. The sessions begin at 8:00 A.M. and end at 5:00 P.M. Scheduling and timing of sessions and breaks are as follows:
  8:00–10:00 A.M., sessions
  10:00–10:30 A.M., break
  10:30–12:00 noon, sessions
  12:00 noon–1:30 P.M., lunch
  1:30–3:00 P.M., sessions
  3:00–3:30 P.M., break
  3:30–5:00 P.M., sessions

Room Setups

For major educational programs of this type, rooms are set theater style, with dual screens and projectors.

All large rooms will have staging, that is, elevated platforms with tables and chairs for speakers, moderators, and co-moderators; the tables will be equipped with microphones for the moderator and co-moderator. Each room will also have a lighted podium equipped with a *lavaliere,* or clip-on, *microphone;* a timer; an electric or laser pointer; and aisle microphones for the audience to step up to and ask questions. The number of aisle microphones will depend on the size of the room.

The Role of an Audiovisual Supervisor

An audiovisual supervisor is responsible for many functions and is the link between a meeting planner and the convention facility, the company supplying the audiovisual equipment, the speakers, and the unions that will be supplying labor for installing and operating the equipment. The supervisor's relationship with the meeting planner is almost identical to that of the show decorator, in that the supervisor, either independently employed or working with an established audiovisual equipment company, enjoys a multiyear contract.

Supervisor Experience

An experienced audiovisual supervisor will save a planner time and, most important, money when renting equipment and scheduling labor for the setup of the meeting rooms, during the show, and during final dismantling of the meeting rooms.

Supervisor Responsibilities

The responsibilities of an audiovisual supervisor, when staging major productions, are as follows:

- Setting up all meeting rooms with adequate screens for optimum viewing

- Ensuring proper sound for maximum understanding of speakers

- Setting up rooms for safety and comfort

- Communicating with all audiovisual personnel and with the facility management to ensure adequate and proper labor during setup, show time, and the dismantling of rooms

- Assisting and educating all speakers in producing a clear, understandable presentation both visually and verbally

- Staffing all meeting rooms with trained audiovisual technicians

- Ensuring that all presentations be delivered on time and according to the printed schedule

Site Evaluation

A site inspection of the facility by the audiovisual supervisor and the meeting planner is typically conducted eighteen months before the show. This inspection gives the facility manager the information necessary to understand the nature of the show (for instance, a technical or medical meeting with extensive audiovisuals versus a more straightforward meeting of antique dealers) and how it will fit into the existing facility. The most recent data on projected attendance, together with last year's specifications for audiovisual equipment and labor, notes about past problems, and information about any unusual characteristics of the group that will affect the overall program, should be discussed.

A word about determining unusual characteristics: An unusual characteristic can be having to redesign a room and its audiovisual equipment in very short order. I recently set up a meeting room with a capacity of two to three thousand people for an opening session and, because of the large number of sessions and lack of other available rooms, had to convert the space immediately into three rooms. That is, in the half hour between session, it was necessary to turn a room for three thousand into three rooms for nine hundred each—complete with audiovisuals—without loss of life or an appearance that all hell was breaking loose. The key to the success of such a colossal switch over is how adept you are at quickly emptying a room with three thousand people—and, of course, planning the choreography well in advance.

After the initial inspection tour and preliminary discussions have been concluded, the audiovisual supervisor will forward to you a set of tentative plans outlining all estimated costs for labor and equipment, as well as questions or suggestions.

Budget

The cost of a fully outfitted room will be based on equipment and labor. The following is an example of a room equipped and staffed for a five-day educational program.

Visual Equipment
2 16-by-16-foot screens @ $150.00	$ 300
2 projectors @ $150.00	300
2 special lenses @ $30.00	60
2 projector stands @ $5.00	10
1 laser pointer @ $70.00	70
1 speaker timer @ $25.00	25

Audio Equipment
M4 microphones @ $45.00   180
Total $945
Labor
  1 operator @ $26.50 per hour × 8 hours × 5 days $1,060

Special lenses are usually employed if the room is large and clarity of image is crucial to the presentation. The figure for labor is variable and will change from city to city and from year to year.

The equipment for this particular room is standard and includes no special video projectors or devices for special effects. Were such equipment used, the rate for this room would be considerably higher and more skilled labor would be needed to operate the equipment at a hourly rate. The minimum cost to operate this particular room throughout a show, however, would be approximately $2,005. ($945 + $1060). This example is a simplification, used merely to demonstrate how basic costs for audiovisuals are determined.

Developing a Flow Chart

The easiest way to cope with the volume of information concerning a large show is to create a flow chart depicted in figure 10–1, annotated to reflect audiovisual details.

    The sample chart below represents one day of a five-day program and will serve as the audiovisual supervisor's foremost guide to everything he or she needs to know for that day's program. For example, by looking at the flow chart the audiovisual supervisor will immediately know how many concurrent sessions are being held—in this case, twelve—which will then automatically indicate the number of operators needed in each meeting room and the number of individual sessions needed to coordinate with the operator of the speaker rehearsal room. Also displayed will be any special video requests or requirements for audiovisual aids like flip charts and overheads. Moreover, the chart will indicate any special sessions in addition to the standard program.

    The flow chart you develop should include all information for all meetings, not just those which are using major audiovisuals. Committee meetings that take place early in the morning, before sessions begin, should be noted. Even though participants did not originally request audiovisual aids, there is always the chance that an overhead or a screen and projector setup will be ordered at the last minute.

Room	120/14/5	123/7	130–132	260/4	261	263/7	264	270	271	274	275
Sq. Ft.	7,740	5,040	12,768	5,040	1,350	5,040	2,520	1,200	1,200	4,256	4,256
Set Theatre	800	500	1,100	500	135	500	250	125	125	400	400
8:30–10:00	session 1 8:45–9:00 ½"VHS	session 2	session 3	no tech.	session 4	session 5	no tech.	session 6	session 7	special session (mics only)	no tech.
10:00–10:30	BREAK	BREAK	special session 10:00–10:30 ½"VHS	BREAK	BREAK	BREAK	BREAK		BREAK	BREAK	BREAK
10:30–12:00	session 8	no tech.	session 9	session 10 10:45–11:00 ¾"VHS	no tech.	session 11	no tech.	no tech.	session 12 10:45–11:00 overhead	no tech.	session 13
12:00–1:30	LUNCH	LUNCH	special session ½"BETA entire session	LUNCH	LUNCH	special session mics only	LUNCH	LUNCH	LUNCH	LUNCH	LUNCH

1:30–3:00	session 14	session 15	session 16 1:30– 1:45 ½"VHS 2:00– 2:15 ½"BETA	session 17	session 18 no tech.	no tech. session 19	overhead entire session session 20
3:00–3:30	BREAK	BREAK	BREAK	BREAK	BREAK	BREAK	BREAK
3:30–5:00	no tech. session 21 3:30– 3:45 ½"VHS 4:00– 4:15 ½"BETA	session 22	session 23	session 24	session 25 no tech.	session 26 no tech.	session 27

Figure 10–1. *Audiovisual flow chart for a convention center representing one day of a meeting. Note how the day is divided into sessions. Audiovisual requirements for the standard room set individually noted*

Note: All rooms are set with dual screen and projection. Technicians are to be present at each session. Special equipment is indicated in each individual session, with time for use. Equipment and technician for special equipment to be present only at stated times.

Schedule Labor

Labor for room setups for audiovisuals come from two sources. First are the audiovisual technicians, usually union, who are hired by the audiovisual supervisor to set up the equipment in the room and, while the program is taking place, to operate the equipment during each session. Second are the people employed by the convention center to set up the nonaudiovisual equipment, such as staging, chairs, and tables for the meeting room.

Whenever information is sent to the audiovisual supervisor, identical information must also be sent to the convention services coordinator at the convention center. Both the audiovisual supervisor and the convention services coordinator must coordinate labor when setting up meeting rooms.

Creating Floor Plans for Meeting Rooms

The audiovisual supervisor will create the floor plans for each meeting room used and will forward them to the convention services coordinator at the convention center. Referring to the flow chart and the floor plans, the convention services coordinator will see when labor will be needed to set up each room. Both the audiovisual supervisor and the convention services coordinator will map out the schedule for labor use. That is, the convention services coordinator will wait for the audiovisual supervisor to set up the screens; then the house crew will set up the chairs, staging, podiums, and so forth and create the aisles; and finally the audiovisual crew will return to set up the projectors, microphones, tape the wires, align the screens, adjust the lights, and test the sound. Figure 10–2, which shows a floor plan set to accommodate two thousand people, lists the equipment needed for a room of this size.

Using the Flow Chart for Move-out

The flow chart can also be used for move-out. If a room is no longer needed, that information is clearly indicated on the chart and the room can be dismantled. If the room has been set up with expensive equipment, quick dismantlement can save money on renting equipment that is no longer needed. With all this information in hand, the audiovisual supervisor will be able to arrive at an accurate estimate of costs for the show.

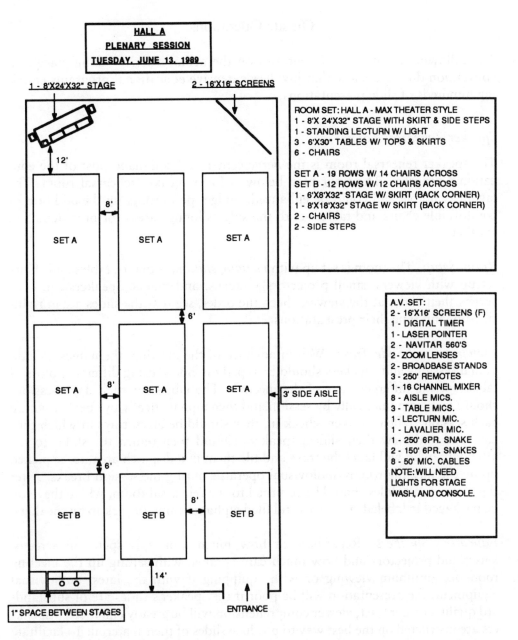

Figure 10–2. *Floor plan of a room set up for two thousand people showing seating arrangement, audiovisual equipment, and staging*

On-site Operations

The following discussion concentrates on the actual activity taking place at a convention during a show that involves extensive educational programs entailing hundreds of slide presentations.

Speaker Rehearsal Room

The speaker rehearsal room is the nerve center and command post of the educational program. The floor plan below is for a speaker rehearsal room. The layout is simple and could be enhanced, budget permitting, by the addition of comfortable chairs and tables set to the side as lounge areas for presenters and speakers.

Room Setup. The room is set up with *viewing stations*—that is, tables and chairs set up with viewers (small projectors), screens, and timers. Speakers can each review their slides at the viewer, check the order, see that the slides are in right-side-up, and time their presentations.

Preparation of Slide Trays. Well in advance of the meeting, the names of individual sessions and speakers should be typed on labels, using different colors of labels for the different days of the meeting. The labels for each day's sessions should be filed numerically by session and then alphabetically by speaker within each session. When speakers check in, they should be given trays in which they can load and view their slides; speakers should then return the slides to the attendant, who will label the trays and file them in a dispatch area, to be picked up by the meeting rooms audiovisual operator during the session breaks. After the sessions, all slides should be returned to the rehearsal room, where they will be packaged in labeled envelopes and filed alphabetically for pickup by speakers.

Educating Speakers. Regardless of how much money is spent on screens, lenses,and projectors and how much care is taken with setting up the meeting room for optimum viewing or with equipping it with the latest audiovisual equipment, the presentation will be poor if the speaker's slides are of substandard quality. By contrast, viewer comprehension will be greatly enhanced if speakers are instructed on the best way to produce slides of their material. To facilitate this educational endeavor, prepare a list of guidelines to send to all speakers before the program. The following letter of instructions is simple and easily understood and, if followed, will result in an excellent presentation.

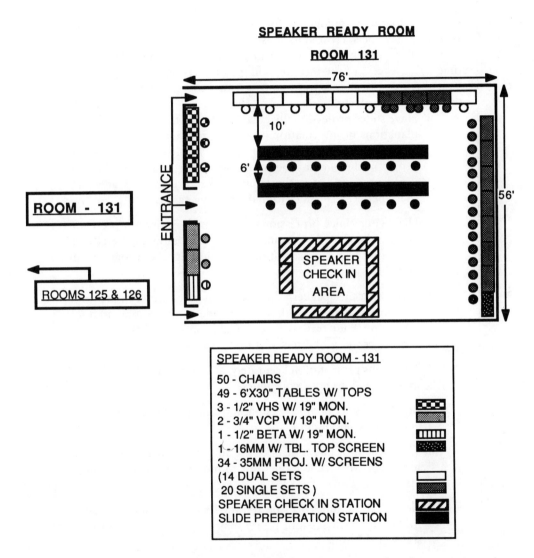

Figure 10–3. *Floor plan of speaker rehearsal room.* Reprinted with permission of Larry Rowell

Memo

To: All speakers
From: Audiovisual supervisor
Re: Guidelines regarding slide preparation and speaker instructions

The following guidelines for slide preparation and speaker instructions have been created to assist you in making a professional presentation of your material at the upcoming meeting in (place, date, time). The success of the meeting will greatly depend on the quality of your slides and your preparation of your oral presentation. Please read the information carefully.

1. Have slides professionally created. Do not try to fit lengthy explanations or information onto one slide. Sentences set in type that is too small, filling up an entire screen, will not be seen by people in the back of the room, no matter how good the projector or how bright the lamp. Make sure there is adequate space between the lines to make reading easier.

2. Have your slides professionally mounted. A smooth presentation can be ruined by jammed, homemade mounts, thereby interrupting your presentation and putting the program off schedule.

3. Please visit the speaker rehearsal room at least two hours prior to your presentation to have your slides properly prepared for projection. Slide trays will be available on-site. Signs in the convention center will direct you to the speaker rehearsal room.

4. Time your presentation accurately, and adhere to your schedule as a courtesy to your colleagues.

5. Before the start of your session, introduce yourself to the moderator or co-moderator.

6. The moderator has control of the automatic timer; thus, watch for a signal from the moderator to indicate when your time is up.

7. Note that all slides will be returned to the speaker rehearsal room after each session. Please make a point to pick up your slides at this time.

8. A trained, experienced technical staff will be available at all times in the speaker rehearsal room to assist you with any prob-

lems or questions. Do not hesitate to call on them; they are there to help you.

9. All rooms will be set up with dual screens and slide projectors, timers, microphones, and pointers. Any additional video equipment or audiovisual aids must be ordered now. Please use the attached order form and mail it to (address) on or before (date); last-minute requests will not be honored.

Audiovisual Needs of Exhibitors

Since may exhibitors use video presentations and slides of their products, they will need projectors, screens, and monitors. By inserting an order form for audiovisual labor and equipment into the exhibitor service kit, you will assist exhibitors in obtaining equipment.

At many large shows, the audiovisual supervisor will set up and staff a portion of the exhibitor's service desk, adjacent to the show decorator's desk, so that an audiovisual technician can assist exhibitors throughout the show.

Knowledge of room setups, screen sizes, and terminology is just part of understanding audiovisual presentations. Actual implementation of a comprehensive audiovisual plan, together with an understanding of the interrelations among the audiovisual supervisor, technicians, convention center staff, speakers, and participants, is the focal point of on-site-audiovisual management.

11
Designing a Shuttle System to Move Thousands

When planning a convention, nothing seems so fraught with confusion as working out the logistics of a shuttle-bus system. Misunderstandings between the meeting planner and the supplier arise when the former has only a sketchy idea of the details involved in developing such a system.

Shuttle systems are expensive, complex, and in most cases necessary. Understanding how suppliers of this service handle the logistics, develop customized schedules for each meeting,and determine costs can help you keep your expenses down and avoid misunderstandings.

Planning a Shuttle System

The planning of a shuttle system often begins twelve to eighteen months before the meeting.

Submitting Information for a Proposal

A shuttle-bus system is only as good as the information you give to the ground operator that will be planning the routes. Insufficient information will be reflected in long lines at the hotels and convention center, missed sessions, and late arrivals at special events.

As the meeting planner, you must outline every detail of the show's schedule, day to day, including evening events and early morning meetings, as well as all hotels that are in the housing block.

Hotels. Begin by listing all hotels in the housing block. Although the format is optional, a chart listing the number of rooms held in each hotel, broken down by the number of singles, doubles, and quads, is the most helpful way to present the information.

The number of rooms you are holding in each hotel will give the ground operator a basic figure with which to begin estimating how many buses will be needed to service that hotel; however, accurate breakdown will make the numbers more realistic.

If, for example, you are holding a block of eight hundred rooms in a hotel and three-quarters of them are doubles, you will be working with a total capacity of approximately fourteen hundred people. If, instead, half the rooms are doubles, total capacity drops to twelve hundred people. This method of analysis should be carried out with every hotel in your block.

Attendee Profile. Providing the ground operator with a profile of your group will refine even further the estimate of the number of people staying at that property.

If your show participants are composed of primarily young adults or perhaps hobbyists who are more likely to double- and quadruple-up in a hotel, your hotel population will increase significantly, in comparison with the numbers for a group of professionals who will be traveling with their spouses and not sharing rooms with other participants.

Distance versus Time

Determining the number of buses needed for each hotel or each bus route is primarily based on the distance of each hotel from the convention center, as well as the number of people who will be using the service in the hotel. In general, the longer the distance and therefore the time it takes to get from the hotel to the convention center, together with the number of people using the shuttle buses in each hotel, the greater the number of buses for that hotel and possibly for that route.

Number of Buses per Hotel. If it takes a bus fifteen minutes to get from the hotel to the convention center and each bus has a capacity of 40 passengers, you can move 40 people to the convention center in fifteen minutes. It will take the bus fifteen minutes more to return to the hotel to pick up another busload of passengers. With this information, you will see that you can move approximately 80 people in an hour. With two buses you will move 160, with three buses, 240, and so on. This example is a simplification, since it would appear that you need seventeen buses on that one route to transport 1,400 people, but you won't. A more detailed explanation of other contributing factors follows.

Number of Buses per Route. The actual number of buses for each route is based on several other variables: the amount of time it takes for each bus to load and unload, the number of buses permitted to park in an area while waiting to be boarded, the hours your program runs, and how efficient the hotel is with moving people. (Even with an adequate number of elevators, it takes time for several hundred people to get to the bus-dispatching area.) Nor will every person who leaves the hotel go to the convention center at the same time. Moreover, it is likely that a substantial number of spouses will remain at the hotel.

Route Plans

The ground operator will try to incorporate several hotels into one bus route if there is a small block in each hotel and if all hotels are on a direct route. What appears to be a natural group of hotels for a bus route may, upon further study, turn out to have its loading and unloading areas on a street that is inaccessible to a bus coming from another hotel—unless, that is, the route is made more complicated by having to circle one or more blocks to approach the loading area. Such a situation will add greatly to the time of the trip for the people who first boarded the bus.

Boarding Areas

Every hotel on the route is restricted to its own and the city's regulations for shuttle boarding areas. Large hotels may designate side or back entrances for buses. Others, even though they are holding a significant block of rooms, must restrict the number of buses in the vicinity of the front entrance to avoid inconveniencing other customers, if these hotels have no side or back entrance.

EPA Standards

In an attempt to improve air-quality levels in major cities, the Environmental Protection Agency (EPA) has placed restrictions on the number of vehicles allowed in specified areas. To facilitate the flow of traffic, the number of waiting buses has been restricted and idling of engines is no longer allowed.

These regulations will have an effect on your bus requirements and will increase the number of buses you will need to service your hotel.

Traffic Patterns

In addition to EPA regulations and allowable loading and unloading areas for hotels and the convention center, bus routes are also affected by traffic patterns during various times of the day. If the convention center is in a downtown area, the buses will be subject to the same kinds of delays that all motorists experience during rush hour.

Convention Center Access

Although many convention centers try to accommodate shuttle buses, they are restricted to the same laws as the rest of the city regarding the idling of engines and the number of waiting buses. The convention centers may also have inadequate loading and unloading areas, a factor that would also restrict the number of buses able to gain access to a center's entrance.

Dispatchers

All good shuttle systems depend on dispatchers to keep the use of buses at peak levels. Each hotel will have one dispatcher monitoring the traffic flow. A well-run system also depends on the communication among dispatchers.

Always in radio contact with one another, dispatchers will be able to determine whether a hotel has cleared most passengers and, listening to transmissions from other hotels' dispatchers, will be able to send surplus buses to help out in those hotels which are moving passengers more slowly—thereby making the most efficient use of all buses.

Off-peak Service

Some meeting planners run shuttle service all day, with a reduction in the number of buses during nonpeak hours, that is, the hours between 10:00 A.M. and 3:00 P.M. Often, the extra buses are used for guest tours.

Coordinators

The efficiency of your shuttle system and the safety of your passengers will depend not only on the dispatchers but also on bus coordinators. These staff members ride the buses from hotels to convention centers, assisting drivers and helping with the loading and unloading of passengers.

Early and Late Events

When working on a bus schedule with your ground operator, pay close attention to both the early morning hours and the after-meeting hours at the convention center. It is easy to forget the needs of members who, in order to attend meetings, may arrive at the center before the programs begin or after they end. If the convention center is not in the heart of town or is in an area that is normally deserted before and after business hours, service should be available.

This type of service rarely includes more than a few buses making a loop from all the hotels to the center.

Signs

The ground operator will develop signs to be placed in each hotel that outline entire convention schedule day by day. In large hotels with many entrances, it is important that each entrance be posted with a sign directing people to the proper entrance for shuttle-bus loading.

In addition to these hotel signs, each bus will have in its front window a sign that clearly states the route number and the association's name. The loading/ unloading area of the convention center, too, will have signs outlining each route and destination.

Shuttle signs, like all signs, represent a fairly substantial expense. The cost is usually outlined in the proposal submitted by the ground operator.

A Typical Schedule

The following schedule for one day during a show is typical of that for a large convention's shuttle system.

Specifications
>The system services five hotels, using two routes.
>
>Route 1 covers four hotels, with the following room blocks:
>
>Hotel 1, 500
>
>Hotel 2, 650
>
>Hotel 3, 350
>
>Hotel 4, 700
>
>Route 2 services one hotel:
>
>Hotel 5, 300
>
>The combined total is 2,500 rooms.
>
>The representative day is day 3 of a five-day show.

Although there are more rooms being served on route one, the turn-round times is minimal due to the proximity of the hotels to the convention center and the directness of the route. Conversely, route two services a hotel farther from the convention center and involves a heavily trafficked course.

Schedule and Service Frequency

Number of Buses	Time	Frequency
Route 1		
6 buses	7:00 A.M.–11:00 A.M.	5–10 minutes
4 buses	11:00 A.M.–3:00 P.M.	10–15 minutes
6 buses	3:00 P.M.–7:00 P.M.	5–10 minutes
Route 2		
3 buses	7:00 A.M.–11:00 A.M.	5–10 minutes
2 buses	11:00 A.M.–3:00 P.M.	10–15 minutes
3 buses	3:00 P.M.–7:00 P.M.	5–10 minutes

Costs

As indicated, the schedule outlined above represents one day in a five-day program. This particular system, depending on the city and the type of buses hired, could cost, anywhere from $25,000 to $35,000.

The actual buses used in this example were air-conditioned motor coaches with upholstered reclining seats. Although some savings could be achieved with less luxurious equipment, that's not always an option.

Typically the cost of the buses, including drivers, is based on a four-hour minimum, with an hourly rate after the minimum is satisfied. In most cases the time is calculated from the buses' departure from the garage, not from the time of arrival at the departure points. Depending on the location, charges are not always suspended for lunch-hour breaks.

To recap, expenses for a total shuttle system will include the following:

- Minimum rate for buses

- Additional hourly rate after the minimum has been satisfied

- Signs

- Off-peak service (optional)

- Walkie-talkies for dispatchers

- Cost of dispatchers, who are usually hired for a minimum number of hours at a specified rate per hour

- Coordination fee of the ground operator (usually a percentage of the total cost)

Evaluating Proposals

Proposals for shuttle service, like those for other convention services, should be based not only on cost but on the reputation of the company supplying the service. Checking references and speaking with other suppliers and the hotels will provide additional insights into the quality of the service.

Quite often the destination management company that is handling the special events for a group is also the supplier for the shuttle service. In this case, reference checking is, of course, simplified.

Deposits

After a ground operator has developed a shuttle system and outlined the costs and fees, it generally requests that you make a deposit by a certain date. Unless the ground operator is a bus company that specializes in shuttle service, it is unlikely that the organization in question will own its own buses.

To protect your interests, you should place a deposit with the company supplying the buses and drivers. Doing so is particularly important in large cities where there are many sightseeing tour programs and even other conventions being held at the same time as yours. New York, San Francisco, and Atlanta are three examples of cities having several arenas and convention facilities that might affect bus availability.

12
A Potpourri of Topics: Ethics, Charting a Career Path in Convention Management, and Organizations and Courses for Meeting Planners

Ethics

The subject of ethics has never been easy, because there is always a great range of opinions as to what makes up ethical behavior. Most would agree that ethics in the workplace requires honesty between people and institutions. This view would certainly apply to meeting planners, who, as purchasers of goods and services, are in a particularly vulnerable position. Meeting planners are actively involved in the decision regarding which city or hotel will receive hundreds of thousands, sometimes millions, of dollars.

The circumstances for bribery or a conflict of interest are therefore ever present. While those two matters are certainly ethical issues, I will assume that anyone who would succumb to such blatantly dishonest acts doesn't read chapters dealing with ethics. The more relevant questions are the borderline gifts and perks that you will most certainly be offered in this industry. And although I would hardly set myself up as the font of wisdom on ethics, I will offer a few thoughts on the subject.

Regarding gifts from hotels and convention and visitors bureaus: If the gift has the name of the city or company written on it and assuming that you can't drive it, swim in it, or wear it on your wrist, it's OK. In other words, if it's not an expensive item and it's a souvenir, don't worry about it.

Another perk often encountered is familiarization trips ("fam trips"). These trips are not all they appear to be to those who aren't meeting planners. It is not unusual for a fam trip to keep a meeting planner running from early morning till late in the evening, inspecting properties and touring cities, with time out for sales presentations. These relationships are truly quid pro quo. The professional meeting planner understands and appreciates the time and effort that go into fam trips and approaches them with the same attitude as any other business meeting.

Decisions about ethical questions are similar to the morals at the ends of 1940s and 1950s B movies that warn against "easy money." If the gift or perk is something wonderful and meaningful to your life and you are now truly happy, give it back. Conversely, if what's being offered is truly meaningless to you, if you no longer have one square inch on your desk left for paperwork because it is covered with paperweights, feel free to accept another paperweight.

I don't mean to trivialize ethics, and I do caution you not to forget the trust that has been placed in you by others. At the same time, agonizing over each chocolate-covered strawberry may be putting too strong an emphasis on nonessentials.

Planning a Career in Convention Management

Convention management is an exciting business, and many people wishing to enter the field will find positions in organizations or associations that stage large annual meetings. Those positions may not be directly related to meeting planning, but the proximity to the meetings department is an inducement to learn more about a meeting planner's work. That knowledge, supplemented by reading trade journals, attending classes on meeting planning, and joining organizations for meeting planners, could result in a meeting-planning job when one becomes available in that company or in another one.

Other job aspirants may be employed as suppliers to the industry—working for hotels, audiovisual companies, or convention and visitors bureaus. For these individuals, making the switch to meeting planning is easier because of the contacts they have established in the industry.

Joining a Professional Organizations

Joining an organization in which the membership consists primarily of meeting planners and suppliers to the industry offers the opportunity to learn the trade or to continue your education in the business as well as develop contacts. The four most well-known associations for meeting planners are the American Society of Association Executives (ASAE), the Professional Convention Management Association (PCMA), Meeting Planners International (MPI), and the National Association of Exhibit Managers (NAEM). These associations offer seminars throughout the year on various aspects of the business, and membership entitles you to receive the organization's magazine. These publications are an excellent source of information about the meeting industry and have many informative articles about meeting planning, convention management, and meeting planners.

For further information on these associations write to the following:

Meeting Planners International
Infomart
1950 Stemmons Freeway
Dallas, TX 75207

American Society of Association Executives
1575 Eye Street NW
Washington, DC 20005

National Association of Exhibit Managers
719 Indiana Avenue
Suite 300
Indianapolis, IN 46202-3135

Professional Convention Management Association
100 Vestavia Office Park, Suite 200
Birmingham, AL 35216

Taking Courses at Colleges and Universities

Over the past few years, many colleges have developed special courses in meeting planning and convention management. Indeed, many of these institutions offer degrees in the subject—which means that the field is becoming more and more complicated and the technical information more voluminous.

The list below outlines some of the schools whose curricula includes meeting planning or convention management. The inclusion of these colleges or the exclusion of others is neither an endorsement nor a condemnation.

Bentley College, Waltham, Massachusetts

Columbia College, Columbia, Missouri

George Washington University, Washington, D.C.

Georgia State University, Atlanta, Georgia

Humber College, Etobicoke, Ontario, Canada

Metropolitan State College, Denver, Colorado

Mt. Hood Community College, Greshen, Oregon

New School for Social Research, New York, New York

New York University, New York, New York

Northeastern State College, Tahlequah, Oklahoma

Northern Virginia Community College, Annandale, Virginia

Orange Coast Community College, Costa Mesa, California

Washington State University at Pullman, Pullman, Washington

Rochester Institute of Technology, Rochester, New York

San Diego Community College, San Diego, California

Sanford Fleming College, Peterborough, Ontario, Canada

University of Central Florida, Orlando, Florida

University of Nevada, Las Vegas, Nevada

Notes

Chapter 1

1. Hosansky, D., "Rust Belt Cities Yearn to Tell a Cinderella Story," *Successful Meetings* 38 (January 1988): 121.

Chapter 2

1. *The Successful Meeting Planner's Handbook,* third ed. Bill Communications, Inc., 1989.

Chapter 4

1. Statistics for door and elevator measurements obtained from *Access New York City, 1981.* Published by the Junior League of the City of New York.

Chapter 5

1. Proposal information courtesy of the Freeman Companies, Houston, TX.

Glossary

1. Some of the terms defined in the glossary are reprinted with the permission of the Convention Liaison Council.

Glossary[1]

This glossary comprises some of the more common terms used in the meeting industry. Although not exhaustive, it will give the reader an opportunity to become familiar with some of the more frequently used terms and phrases.

Airport shuttle   As used in this book, the phrase *airport shuttle* refers to the system that returns attendees to the airport directly from the convention center, thereby eliminating a return to various hotels to collect luggage.

Air wall   Movable wall or barrier dividing a large meeting room into two or several smaller rooms. These walls are not always soundproof. A soundproofing solution would be to run two parallel walls to create an empty corridor between two rooms to muffle sound.

Aisle signs   Informational or directional signs suspended from ceiling grids.

All-space hold   Function and meeting space held at a hotel for the exclusive use of a group.

Ambient light   Natural or unavoidable light. An audiovisual term referring to light from around doors or draped windows seeping into a dark room.

Audiovisual supervisor   The person responsible for coordinating various tasks necessary to the setting up of all audiovisual requirements at a meeting or convention, including educational programs, exhibitor orders, and other on-site communication. The audiovisual supervisor is the link between (a) the meeting planner, the convention center management, the show decorator, and labor and (b) all stagehands, operators, and other audiovisual personnel.

Baffle   A screen or partition used to block sound or ambient light or to help control traffic flow.

Bank Maze   Posts and ropes set up to control traffic and crowding in registration or other lines.

Bill of lading   A form listing the exhibitor's or shipper's goods and stating the terms, shipping arrangements, and type of merchandise.

Blanket-wrap merchandise   Exhibit material that cannot be crated. Delicate or expensive equipment that needs special care is blanket wrapped for shipment. Common carriers do not normally handle blanket-wrap merchandise; van lines are employed for such freight—a more expensive way to ship.

Boardroom   A meeting room with a stationary table; sometimes this factor is not noted on hotel floor plans.

Boneyard   On-site storage area for audiovisual, decorator, and other supplier materials.

Breakdown   Dismantling of a meeting room, exhibit hall, or function space.

Breakout rooms   Small meeting rooms, usually near a large function room in a meeting area.

Breakout sessions   Sessions, usually held after a general meeting, in which specific tasks or missions are assigned to individual groups established at a general session.

Call brands   Selection of liquor by brand, according to customer preference.

Cancellation clause   Outline of terms regarding penalties if either party fails to comply with contractual terms.

Capacity   Maximum number of persons allowed in a meeting room or function area, as established by the local fire marshal.

Cash bar   Bar setup in which attendees pay for their own drinks.

Chaser lights   Lights that flash in a sequential pattern.

Column   A support pillar in a building. When reviewing floor plans of an exhibit hall, note that a pillar is indicated by a solid square.

Common carrier   Transportation company that moves merchandise over land or sea or by air. Generally, common carriers will ship exhibits only if they are crated. Several different exhibits can be transported in one shipment if crated individually, reducing costs to individual exhibitors.

Communications center   An office set up at a convention site to coordinate and relay information.

Complimentary rooms   Number of rooms a hotel will provide without charge on the sale of rooms in a room block. A typical complimentary room allocation arrangement is one complimentary room for every fifty rooms sold.

Conference style   A room set up with all attendees sitting around a table.

Contractor   Person or company supplying services and goods to show management or exhibitors.

Convention and visitors bureau   Usually a city- or state-operated organization offering information and services for meeting planners and convention managers.

Corkage fee   Fee charged for glasses, ice, and service when a meeting planner brings beverages into a hotel or other facility.

Corner booth   An exhibit bordered by two aisles at a cross-aisle point.

Crash door   A door that can be opened by pushing a waist-high bar extending the width of the door. Used in theaters, ballrooms, arenas, or anywhere large numbers of people congregate. Facilitates quick exiting in an emergency.

Cutoff date   The date a hotel will release any unsold rooms in a block for sale to the general public.

Dead space   An audiovisual term relating to an area in a meeting room or indoor space where sound is unclear or absent.

Delegate   Meeting attendee with voting rights. Sometimes the term is used to describe all convention attendees, whether voting or nonvoting.

Destination management company   Company offering assistance to meeting planners for ground operations, shuttle service, management of special events, party decorations, and entertainment.

Direct billing   Method used by a hotel or other facility to establish credit with a client and bill all goods and services on one account, with a postmeeting billing date. This method eliminates on-site payment.

Dispatcher   Person in charge of routing and scheduling of labor, freight, and shuttle buses.

Drayage   Movement of freight from point of arrival to exhibit space or other areas of the exhibit hall. Drayage also includes removal and return of empty crates to the exhibit space and other areas after the show.

Elevation   Drawing depicting front and side views of an exhibit.

Empties   Crates after removal of exhibit material.

Empty labels   Labels placed on empties for storage and identification.

Event orders   Instruction sheet, usually generated by the convention services manager in a hotel or convention center, detailing all aspects of an event—food-and-beverage requirements, room setups, and scheduling. Sometimes referred to as a function sheet or résumé.

Exclusive contractor   The only service or merchandise vendor allowed to (a) operate at a facility or (b) service a particular show. The first is determined by the facility management; the second, by the show manager.

Exhibit manager   (a) Person in charge of an individual exhibit or (b) show management.

Exhibitor Preview meeting   Meeting arranged by convention management to introduce suppliers and exhibitors.

Exhibitor prospectus   A sales and marketing document sent by show management to prospective exhibitors.

Exhibitor service kit   Packet, folder, or manual sent to all participating exhibitors and containing show rules and regulations and order forms for labor, services, and equipment.

Exposition manager   Staff member of exhibiting organization who is in charge of the entire convention.

Fam trip   Familiarization tour of a facility or location to determine its suitability as a meeting or convention site.

Feedback   An audiovisual term used to describe a return flow of sound into a room from amplifying equipment. Usually a loud noise.

First-, second, and third-tier cities   Designations used to describe a city's level of services and facilities as related to conventions and meetings.

Flip chart   Large pad mounted on an easel.

Floaters   Workers used by supervisors to help labor for short periods of time.

Floor load   Maximum weight per square foot a floor can support. Can also refer to the maximum amount of power available from electrical floor outlets.

Floor order   Call for services or labor on the exhibit floor, usually by an exhibitor. More costly than ordering in advance of setup.

Floor plan   Design of a room or an entire exhibit floor, including dimensions and placement of obstructions (pillars, columns, electrical outlets, and so on).

Floor port   In an exhibit hall, a recessed area containing a utility box for electrical, plumbing, or phone connections.

Folio   Individual charge accounts (a) for guests or (b) within one master account.

Force majeure   Standard contract clause exempting either party from liability for nonfulfillment of services or obligations owing to acts of God or conditions beyond the party's control.

Forklift Motorized vehicle with a pronged platform, power operated, used to life or carry crates or other material.

Four-hour call Under certain circumstances, the minimum work period for which union labor must be paid.

Front projection Audiovisual method in which an image is projected to the front of the screen (the projector is at the back of the room). See *rear projection*.

Function sheet See *event orders*.

Gross square footage Entire space of an exhibit hall.

Ground operator Company that handles arrangements for land transportation.

Guarantee Number of servings to be paid for at a function having food-and-beverage offerings; the number that will be paid for whether provisions are consumed or not.

Header Overhead, illuminated display sign, sometimes referred to as facia.

Headquarters Hotel chosen as the site for all social activity during a convention.

Hollow square Room setup in which tables are arranged to crate a square or rectangle) with seating around the outside of the square. Employed when conference style is wanted but the group is too large to accommodate it.

Hospitality suite In a hotel or convention center, a room used to serve refreshments to meeting attendees. Usually such gatherings are hosted by exhibitors.

Hosted bar Bar setup in which refreshments are paid for by the host or sponsor of the bar; opposite of cash bar.

House brand Moderately priced brands of liquor chosen by a facility.

Housing block (a) Number of sleeping rooms held by a hotel for an organization's exclusive use. (b) Entire number of rooms held in a number of hotels.

Housing bureau Service maintained by a convention and visitors bureau to help meeting planners with housing for groups. A housing bureau will process all housing requests, assign rooms, create reports, and oversee room distribution pertaining to a convention's housing block.

Housing form Form used by attendees and exhibitors to request housing.

Incidentals Guest expenses other than those for room and tax.

Independent service contractor Any company (other than those designated official contractors in the exhibitor service kit) providing a service (I & D, florist, photographer, audiovisual, and so on) that requires access to the exhibit hall.

Installation and Dismantle (I & D)   Phrase referring to the building and breaking down of an exhibition or individual exhibit.

Island exhibit   Sometimes called island display, booth, or free-form exhibit. Refers to a free-standing structure that is bordered by aisles only.

Junior suite   Large room partitioned to separate sleeping area from sitting area.

King   Room with a king-size bed

Kit   See *exhibitor service kit.*

Labor call   (a) Method of securing union labor; (b) time specified for labor to report, as in a 7:00 A.M. labor call; or (c) minimum amount for which labor must be paid (see *four-hour call*).

Labor desk   See *service desk.*

Lavaliere microphone   A small microphone that clips onto a speaker's lapel.

Lead list   List of attendees at a trade show, generated on-site for use by exhibitors to follow up on contacts made at the show.

Liability   The state of being responsible for damage or injury.

Linear displays   Exhibits or displays arranged in a straight line.

Loading dock   Area of a facility where freight is received or sent.

Local   Local labor union affiliated with a national or international union.

Marshaling yard   Area where trucks are held until the loading dock area is free.

Masking drape   Drape used to screen messy or unsightly areas.

Master account   Account at a hotel or facility whereby all expenses are charged.

Meeting specifications   A description of an entire meeting, outlining specific needs. Usually sent by a meeting planner to suppliers or vendors when the planner requests a proposal for services.

Message center   Desk set up on-site for use by attendees to receive or leave messages.

Modular exhibit   An exhibit composed of various components that are intechangeable, affording flexibility in size and arrangement.

Move-in   Beginning of a show's installation or date on which an exhibition is scheduled to begin installation.

Move-out   Date scheduled for dismantling an exhibition or actual process of dismantling.

Multi-story exhibit   Two-story exhibit, sometimes referred to as a double-decker.

Net square footage   Space occupied by an exhibit on the exhibit floor.

No-show   Exhibition: Exhibitors who do not show up to set up their exhibit or use labor and services that were ordered. Meeting: A registrant who does not appear. Hotel: A guest who has made a reservation but does not appear.

Office central   An office set up and staffed by the exhibiting organization where attendees and staff can report problems or seek assistance.

Official contractor   Supplier of services or merchandise or a company designated by show management to provide services to show management and exhibitors (not to be confused with exclusive contractor).

One-for-fifty (1/50)   Hotel term describing the complimentary room policy.

On-site order   Same as floor order.

On-site registration   Method used when attendees register at the site of a convention.

Open bar   see *hosted bar.*

Overbooking   In hotel terminology, the practice of confirming more sleeping rooms than are actually available, so as to protect against loss of revenue from no-shows.

Overflow housing   Any hotel in the housing block used to only house delegates. Not the headquarter hotel.

Overtime (OT) labor   Labor performed overtime, at either time-and-a-half or double the standard rate.

Pallet   Wooden platform onto which goods are loaded.

PBX operator   Switchboard operator

Peninsula exhibit   An exhibit with aisles on three sides.

Perimeter booth   A booth or exhibit located on an outside wall.

Pickup   Hotel term referring to the number of rooms or room nights sold.

Pipe and drape   Tubing, usually plastic, from which draping is hung to separate booths, hide storage areas, create rails, or divide rooms.

Plenary session   Usually the opening meeting of an exhibition, one in which all participants are assembled.

Point priority system   System established by exhibit management to assign booth space on the exhibit floor.

Postcon (postconvention) meeting   Follow-up meeting held after a convention to critique overall performance and results.

Poster presentation   Material displayed on a poster board. Quite often used at educational meetings as a teaching device.

Precon (preconvention) meeting   Meeting held a day or two prior to an exhibition's opening day and attended by all major suppliers of goods and services and by facility and show management in order to finalize last-minute details and coordination of the event.

Prefab   An exhibit that has been previously built and is ready for installation when it arrives on the exhibit floor.

Prefunction space   The area near the site of a main event or the area immediately outside a ballroom.

Premium brands   The most expensive brands of liquor and beer at a facility.

Preregistration   Process of registering before an event—completing paperwork and mailing forms to exhibit management to avoid registering onsite.

Preset   (a) Audiovisual term referring to lighting in meeting rooms and (b) food-and-beverage term referring to placing food on tables before guests are seated.

Press kit   A folder or manual, prepared for distribution to the press, containing literature about a product or company.

Press release   A specific article released to the media about a product, company, service, or person connected with an exhibition.

Pressroom   Room set up for representatives of TV and other media.

Property removal pass   Pass required by security personnel from an exhibitor or any other person taking material from the exhibit floor.

Proposal   An offering of goods and/or services, usually made in response to a meeting planner's request for a proposal and the planner's submission of a list of specifications.

Public show   A show attended by the general public.

Quad   Sleeping room with two or more beds for four people.

Qualifying leads   The process used by exhibitors to determine whether a booth visitor is qualified to purchase merchandise or devices or has a part in the purchase decision-making process.

Queen-room   Sleeping room with a queen-size bed.

Rack rate   Hotel term referring to the posted rate of sleeping rooms.

Rear projection   Audiovisual method in which the projector is behind the screen (at the front of the room). A more expensive alternative to front projection, in which the image is projected in front of the screen and the projector is in the back of the room, behind the audience.

Rebate   Money returned to an organization after having been added to rooms or services, over and above the negotiated rate.

Registrar   Show personnel responsible for registering attendees.

Request for a proposal   A statement of activity developed by a meeting planner; used when seeking bids from services from suppliers.

Riser   Platform built to elevate persons or products in a meeting room or exhibit hall. See also *staging*.

Room block   Number of rooms being held by a hotel for a group.

Room nights   Number of rooms sold multiplied by the number of nights occupied. For example: Twenty rooms occupied for three nights equals sixty room nights.

Rounds   Round banquet tables, usually set for seating eight (or sometimes ten persons).

Schoolroom style   Meeting room set up with tables and chairs, one behind the other, as in a schoolroom.

Security cage   Secured cage, either stationary or movable, for storage of equipment.

Self-contained exhibit   An exhibit or display in which the crating or shipping case becomes part of the unit.

Seminar   A supervised study group, usually allowing group interaction and featuring an expert lecturer.

Service desk   Desk located on an exhibit floor for the purpose of enabling exhibitors to order labor, services, utilities, and materials.

Service kit   See *exhibitor service kit*.

Set up   Meeting: How a meeting or function room is furnished or the actual process of furnishing. Food and beverage: A bar set up for service with glasses, mixers, fruit, and so forth.

Shuttle-bus system   Bus routes servicing hotels and the convention center.

Show decorator   The person, hired by show management, who is responsible for decorating and servicing an entire show. Show decorators are also used by individual exhibitors to install, decorate, and dismantle booths and exhibits. A show decorator is sometimes referred to as a service contractor or general contractor.

Show manager   See *exposition manager.*

Side rail   Divider, usually constructed of pipe and drape, separating one exhibit space from another.

Site inspection   Tour conducted by a meeting planner to evaluate a city, facility, or area.

Skid   See *pallet.*

Skirting   Material or decorative covering around risers or staging, used to hide an unsightly support structure. In audiovisual terminology, material hung around or at the bottom of screens to hide screen supports or to create a movie-house effect for rear screen projection.

Sound mixing   Audiovisual phrase referring to the process of combining separately recorded material onto a master tape.

Speaker rehearsal room   Room furnished with video equipment, viewers, projectors, and slide trays for use by speakers to rehearse their presentations, load slide trays, and prepare slides.

Sponsor   An exhibitor who will pay for an event, service, or merchandise in return for acknowledgment.

Sponsorship   Any item, service, or event funded by an exhibitor.

Spouse tours/programs   Educational or special events developed for the spouses of meeting attendees.

Staging   (a) producing an event or (b) platform (see *riser*).

Strike   (a) In exhibit terminology, dismantling of exhibits; (b) in audiovisual terminology, breakdown of all audiovisual equipment ("to strike a room"); and (c) walkout of union labor during a show.

Subcontractor   Company or person hired by a service contractor (show decorator) to provide services.

Suite   One or more bedrooms connected to a parlor.

Supervisor   Person who organizes and directs labor on the exhibit floor.

Supplier   Seller of goods and/or services.

Symposium   See *seminar.*

Tabletop display   Usually, a small exhibit designed to fit on a table, with or without a booth.

Task lighting   Low-level lighting in a darkened meeting room, used for safety and for taking notes.

Tear down   To dismantle, strike.

Theater style   Meeting room set up with rows of chairs (as in a theater), with no tables, with or without staging, but usually with a head table and/or podium.

Theme party   Party or event where decorations, food, music, and other entertainment are all based on one theme or motif.

Ticketed event   A party or event whereby all attendees must present a ticket in order to be admitted.

Trade show   Exposition produced for people with a common interest. Not open to the general public.

Traffic flow   Pattern that attendees will take through an exhibit hall.

Truck entries   Large entries or large runways giving access directly onto the exhibit floor.

Turndown service   In hotel terminology, an amenity offered by some hotels, wherein the bed covers are turned down and sometimes chocolates are left on the bedside table or on the pillow. The service may also include refreshing the bathroom and adding clean towels.

Twin   A guest room with two single beds.

Upgrade   To move a guest or client to a better class of room or service, with no increase in cost.

User meeting   Exhibitor meeting organized for attendees for the purpose of educating clients and prospects about the product or service.

Value season   Phrase used by some hotels and suppliers to indicate off-peak season, affording the purchaser lower prices.

Vendor   See *supplier*.

Viewing station   Tables and chairs set up with slide viewers and screens in a speaker rehearsal room.

Walk   Hotel term referring to the disposition of guests. Guests with confirmed reservations at a hotel are either turned away or "walked" to another hotel because of overbooking of a facility or because expected guest departures did not occur as planned.

Walk-through   Detailed inspection of a facility (a) before the installation of an exhibition, to ascertain the condition of the building and to note preexisting damage, or (b) after the exposition or convention, to ascertain damage occurring during the show.

Workshop   Instruction for a small, supervised group, sometimes including hands-on exercises, in order to enhance skills or teach new procedures in a specific area.

Suggested Reading List

Fundamentals of Association Management: Conventions. Published by the American Society of Association Executives (ASAE) in 1985, this book is a compilation of articles previously published in ASAE's monthly magazines. It offers a good overview of the industry. For information about this title write to ASAE, 1575 Eye Street, Washington, DC 10005.

PCMA Professional Meeting Management: The Complete Guide to Convention and Meeting Planning. Edited by Barbara Nichols and published by the Professional Convention Management Association (PCMA) of Birmingham, Alabama, this guide covers everything—from small groups and conventions to meetings on cruise ships. The information was compiled by suppliers and other people active in the industry, i.e., convention and visitor's bureau representatives, audiovisual company executives, hotel sales and catering representatives, decorating company representatives, and meeting planners. All the detail is here, although much of it is unnecessary unless you plan to take on chores single-handedly. The lack of an index and glossary weakens an otherwise good resource book.

Annual Guide to Exposition Services. Published jointly by the National Association of Exposition managers, Inc. (NAEM) and the Exposition Service Contractors Association (ESCA), this is a resource book for meeting planners with information on suppliers and facilities. The guide lists major convention centers and includes all union rules and regulations as well as fire laws for individual facilities. Although it is not intended as an instructional book, the guide helps familiarize meeting planners with complex union rules and trade terminology.

Index

About the Author

Michele Voso has been a meeting planner and convention manager for nine years. She got her start in writing by working as a reporter and assistant to the editor for the *Guinness Book of World Records*. She is currently the convention manager for a large medical association and is assistant adjunct professor at New York University where she teaches convention management.